D0145412

EMPIRE AND NATION

Empire and Nation

Letters from a Farmer in Pennsylvania

John Dickinson

Letters from the Federal Farmer

Richard Henry Lee

Second Edition

Edited by Forrest McDonald

Liberty Fund
Indianapolis

This book is published by Liberty Fund, Inc., a foundation established to encourage study of the ideal of a society of free and responsible individuals.

The cuneiform inscription that serves as our logo and as the design motif for our endpapers is the earliest-known written appearance of the word "freedom" (*amagi*), or "liberty." It is taken from a clay document written about 2300 B.C. in the Sumerian city-state of Lagash.

First published in 1962 by Prentice-Hall, Inc.

Printed in the United States of America

Library of Congress Cataloging-in-Publication Data
Empire and nation / edited by Forrest McDonald.—2nd ed.
p. cm.
Contents: Letters from a farmer in Pennsylvania / John Dickinson —Letters from the Federal farmer / Richard Henry Lee.
Includes bibliographical references.
ISBN 0-86597-202-8 (alk. paper).—ISBN 0-86597-203-6 (pbk. : alk. paper)
1. United States—History—Revolution, 1775–1783—Causes. 2. Great Britain—Colonies—America—Administration. 3. Great Britain—Colonies—America—Economic policy. 4. United States. Constitution. 5. United States. Constitutional Convention (1787) I. Dickinson, John, 1732–1808. Letters from a farmer in Pennsylvania. II. Lee, Richard Henry, 1732–1794. III. McDonald, Forrest.
E215.5.E4 1999
973.3′11—dc21 98-2833

03 02 01 00 99 C 5 4 3 2 1
03 02 01 00 99 P 5 4 3 2 1

Liberty Fund, Inc.
8335 Allison Pointe Trail, Suite 300
Indianapolis, IN 46250-1687

Contents

Preface to the Liberty Fund Edition

A minor problem arises in connection with the decision to reissue the classic essays in this volume, one that at first blush may seem not minor at all. Richard Henry Lee's authorship of the *Letters from the Federal Farmer* has been questioned. It had, indeed, been challenged even before my first edition appeared in 1962. William W. Crosskey, an erratic and controversial constitutional historian, declared flatly in a 1953 book, *Politics and the Constitution,* that Lee was not the author, but he did not develop the assertion. He promised to discuss the matter fully in a subsequent work, but he died before that work was finished. More recently, in 1974, Gordon Wood published an article in the *William and Mary Quarterly,* in which he analyzed the internal logic of the letters and compared them with other examples of Lee's writings. Wood concluded that there is no definite proof that Lee is the author, despite historians' repeated attribution of the letters to him.

Although Lee apparently never claimed authorship—which was not uncommon among anonymous pensmen—he never denied it, either. Moreover, he was widely assumed at the time to have been the Farmer. At least ten writers (themselves anonymous) asserted in newspapers from New England to Georgia that the letters were Lee's. Conceding that the question cannot be definitively answered unless new evidence turns up, I nonetheless share the view of his contemporaries.

I said that the point is a minor one. In a sense, it does not matter if the author is Lee or someone else. The Richard Henry Lee I describe in the introduction was a real person, but he was also a type that was especially widespread among Virginians of the revolutionary generation: my words could be applied to scores of public men; the names of James Monroe, William Grayson, Arthur Lee, George Wythe, and most of the more ideological anti-Federalist members of the Virginia ratifying convention come immediately to mind. The very fact that the mode of thinking and the ideas about government expressed by the Federal Farmer were in common currency helps explain why the letters were so influential at the time—and why they are of enduring value to those who would understand the framing.

Another prefatory note wants making. In the introduction, I depict John Dickinson and Richard Henry Lee as being poles apart in their approaches to politics and government. And so they were; but viewed from a different perspective they appear as one. Like other leaders during the founding of the American nation, they were imbued with an abiding love of liberty and a concomitant wholesome distrust of government. Those attributes guided their every public word and deed, and we owe them mightily.

Introduction

At first glance, it might seem that John Dickinson's *Letters from a Farmer in Pennsylvania* and Richard Henry Lee's *Letters from the Federal Farmer* have little in common beyond being epistles from negative-minded agrarians. Two decades and a Revolution separated their publication: Dickinson's *Letters* were published late in 1767, Lee's late in 1787. Their subject matter appears even less related, for Dickinson wrote in opposition to the Townshend Acts, Lee in opposition to the ratification of the Constitution of the United States. Finally, though both men rank among the more celebrated of the Founding Fathers, they stood on opposite sides of the two most important issues of the revolutionary epoch. In the summer of 1776 Lee authored the motion that the colonies should sever their ties with Britain, and Dickinson was among the foremost opponents of the Declaration of Independence. Eleven summers later, Dickinson helped author the Constitution, and Lee was among its foremost opponents.

But in fact they are dealing with the same question, the never-ending problem of the distribution of power in a broad and complex federal system. Despite a persistent myth of a bygone *laissez-faire* paradise (or hell, depending on the point of view), Americans have always been accustomed to fairly extensive governmental interference in their lives, but they have continually argued over just which government should do the interfering. When the British government began to levy taxes on the colonies, when the colonies declared their independence, when the new states joined in a "league of friendship" under the Articles of Confederation, when they formed a "more perfect union" under the Constitution, the sum total of governmental power that was recognized as legitimate remained essentially the same. What was being changed was the distribution of power, the equilibrium of the federal system. And each time power has shifted, from then until now, Americans have re-argued the question.

As documents that shaped opinion on two critical attempts to relocate power, Dickinson's and Lee's letters are historically significant, but they are at least equally significant as archetypes. Dickinson's view is historical, pragmatic, and in the Burkean sense, conservative; Lee's is immediate, rational, and in the Jeffersonian sense, liberal. Throughout his life, Dickinson explicitly rejected the rationalism of the eighteenth century; "Experience," he once said, "must be our only guide," for "reason may mislead us." As consistently, Lee defended the possibility of a clean, rational break with the past. Because these two attitudes form the principal molds into which Americans have cast their arguments over the location of power—as well as over most other political questions—Dickinson and Lee may well be regarded as models for the American political tradition.

John Dickinson was not, strictly speaking, either a farmer or a Pennsylvanian. He was born in Maryland (1732), grew up and received a thorough education in classics and history in Delaware (1742–53), studied law at the Middle Temple in London (1753–57), then returned and was admitted to the bar in Philadelphia. He rapidly attained a lucrative and prestigious practice; almost as rapidly, he succumbed to the lure of politics, the occupational hazard of lawyers in a popular government. In 1760 he became a member of the Assembly of Delaware, and two years later he was elected to the Assembly of Pennsylvania (until the Revolution, Pennsylvania and Delaware were not entirely separate: they had individual legislatures but a common governor). During most of his remaining life he practiced law in Philadelphia, maintained a country estate in Delaware, and was active in the politics of both colonies/states.

His first major action in Pennsylvania politics demonstrated the stand he was to take all his life, and incidentally won him brief but widespread unpopularity. In 1764 Benjamin Franklin and Joseph

Galloway led a movement to have the Penns' proprietary charter revoked, and thus to transform Pennsylvania into a royal colony. The colonists had abundant grievances against the proprietary governor, and few save Dickinson were willing to take a strong stand against Franklin and Galloway. But Dickinson was instinctively wary of any sudden, decisive action, and he knew too much British history to believe that kings and ministers were repositories of infinite virtue, and so he fought. Within eighteen months his argument—that, bad as the proprietors were, the charter did guarantee certain liberties, and Pennsylvanians had no reason to expect improvement by entrusting themselves to the king and his ministers—proved prophetic. In 1765 the Grenville ministry produced the Stamp Act, and subsequent ministries produced the succession of acts that became stepping stones to revolution.

For the next decade, circumstances placed a premium on Dickinson's particular combination of attitudes and talents. For centuries Englishmen had, when considering something new in politics, justified their espousal (or opposition) by maintaining that they sought only to restore (or preserve) something that Englishmen had always had. Now, in the vast imperial constitutional crisis of 1765–76, the Americans needed a spokesman who could, in this traditional way, justify their resistance to British authority. Whatever their motives for resisting—and these ranged from such sordid aims as grabbing land, repudiating personal debts, and smuggling, to idealistic concern for the supposed natural rights of man—Americans needed someone who could state their case in such a way as to make king and parliament out as radical innovators, and themselves out as defenders of ancient traditions. This, in fact, is just what Dickinson believed to be the case, and few colonists so believing could match Dickinson's knowledge of history and law and his skill with words.

From the Stamp Act Congress (at which he wrote the celebrated resolutions declaring Britain had no right to tax the colonies) until the eve of the Second Continental Congress, Dickinson's was among the most eloquent and respected voices in the colonies. Such was the respect he commanded by 1776 that he could refuse to vote for or sign the Declaration of Independence—for the same conservative, pragmatic, and historical reasons that he opposed the Stamp Act—and yet continue to be generally regarded as a patriot.

This enormous prestige was built largely upon the *Letters from a Pennsylvania Farmer.* The immediate background of these essays lay in two loosely connected sets of events. The first was an act, passed at about the time of the Stamp Act, that required each colony to furnish food and shelter for soldiers stationed within its boundaries; this did not tax the colonies, but it required them to tax themselves. To hedge on this issue while contesting the larger issue of parliament's right to tax directly, most colonies were careful to comply only in part or to offer the services as a voluntary gift, making no reference to the parliamentary law. New York, which had more troops than anyone else, flatly refused to comply, and its assembly was prorogued, an action that took some of the luster from the victory the colonies were winning in the Stamp Act controversy.

The other set of events was the Declaratory Act and the Townshend Acts. In March, 1766, parliament repealed the Stamp Act, but not without simultaneously declaring that it had the right to legislate for the colonies "in all cases whatsoever." Fifteen months later, it passed the Townshend Acts, imposing duties to be paid by the colonists on certain items they imported (paper, glass, lead, paints, tea), and reorganizing the entire colonial customs machinery—an action which one historian has called "England's most fateful action."

In taking these steps, Britain was making the most dangerous of all political blunders: it was stating its position clearly and as an absolute. Until that moment, the imperial system had worked, and it had worked precisely because it had never been clearly defined. Now, parliament was declaring, in effect, "This is what the empire is, and this is what it shall be." The Stamp Act had been easy for the colonists to react to, for it was gross, and resisting it necessitated no final commitment on the nature of the imperial system. The Declaratory and Townshend Acts were the opposite: the taxes imposed were subtle, being small and painlessly collected, but resisting them was an irreversible step. In 1765, the tax issue had been clear and the imperial issue muddled; in 1767, it was the other way around. Small wonder that the colonists hesitated before taking their stand.

For once, Dickinson hesitated not at all; or if he did, it was only long enough to learn whether anyone else would take up the gauntlet, and no longer. By the time the new customs commissioners arrived in America, Dickinson had his twelve epistolary essays ready as a greeting of unwelcome. He dated his first letter November 5, 1767, the seventy-ninth anniversary of the landing of William the Third at Torbay, the occasion that "gave Constitutional Liberty to all Englishmen." The letters were published in twelve installments in the weekly *Pennsylvania Chronicle and Universal Advertiser*, beginning with the issue of November 30. Their impact and their circulation were unapproached by any publication of the revolutionary period except Thomas Paine's *Common Sense*. (Indeed, because they were a crucial step toward transforming the mass circulation pamphlet into the soberest forum for debating public issues, they helped make *Common Sense* possible.) They were quickly reprinted in newspapers all over the colonies, and published in pamphlet form in Philadelphia (three editions), Boston (two editions), New York, Williamsburg, London, Paris, and Dublin. Immediately, everyone took Dickinson's argument into account: Americans in assemblies, town meetings, and mass meetings adopted resolutions of thanks; British ministers wrung their hands; all the British press commented, and a portion of it applauded; Irish malcontents read avidly; even the dilettantes of the Paris salons discussed the Pennsylvania Farmer.

But the consequences were a good deal more important than just that. Parliament had posed a rigid, narrow, arbitrary definition of its powers; Dickinson countered with a subtle, pluralistic, historical, realistic definition of the imperial constitution; but his view was, in its way, as brittle and as absolute as was parliament's. Parliament's claim admitted only of acceptance or rejection; Dickinson pleaded for conciliation, flexibility, mutual concession, but by the very act of attempting to pin down the location of power in the empire, he reduced the empire to a form in which concession was impossible. In the long run, Dickinson's system admitted no more of compromise than did parliament's. Together, they forced everyone on both sides to face and give a firm answer to a forbidden question: what is the nature and distribution of power in the imperial system? To force a firm answer to that question was to invite destruction, for the only viable federal system is one in which power is free to shift.

Richard Henry Lee—a Virginia aristocrat who was, like Dickinson, born in 1732—was a weaker and more attractive breed of man. He was as rash as Dickinson was prudent, as flamboyant as Dickinson was straightlaced, as cunning as Dickinson was straightforward. Both got into political hot water from time to time, but when Dickinson did so, his action usually reeked of integrity, and when Lee did so his action usually smacked of the unsavory.

The most significant differences were two. The first was that mentioned earlier: that Dickinson was in the historical and Lee was in the rationalist tradition. In the historical view, men have such rights as they have won over the years; in the rationalist view, men are born with certain rights, whether they are honored in a particular society or not. The other difference lay in their talents for expressing themselves. Dickinson wrote extremely well, but was a mediocre speaker; Lee was a mediocre writer and a brilliant orator. Dickinson's influence was felt wherever men could read; Lee's was confined to the range of his own voice, and so in the decade before independence, when Dickinson's word reached everyone, Lee's scarcely reached across the Potomac.

But there soon came a day when the voice spoke louder than the pen. Amid the smoke and flames of 'seventy-five and 'seventy-six, in the halls of the first and second Continental Congresses, Lee and his cohort Patrick Henry and their kindred soul Sam Adams seized leadership. By their shrewd maneuvers and their ringing appeals to the rights of man, they swayed the men who held the fate of the colonies in their hands, and thus brought revolution where those like Dickinson had sought stability.

In another decade, Dickinson and his kind had their day again: in 1787, they wrote the Constitution of the United States. This occasioned for Lee—as it did for several of his friends of 1776—the last great political battle of his life.

The Constitution located power not only in a new place but also in a new way, and for each reason it encountered a ready-made set of enemies. It took some (but not all) powers then being exercised by the states, shifted them upstream, and thereby created a new general government. Automatically, almost everyone with a vested interest, political or economic, in the system of the Articles of Confederation—under which the states were all-but-sovereign republics—fought the change. At the same time the Constitution relocated power, it distributed the new national power among three branches of government; but at each axis the lines of separation were left blurred, shifting, and sometimes nonexistent. The result was a most irrational (and therefore viable) system: a many-faceted government in which it was impossible to pin down the location of power. Automatically, almost all rationalists—most of whom were republican idealogues—also fought the change.

Even before the Constitution appeared in September, 1787, Lee stood poised, pen in hand, ready to attack it. A believer in a national government founded on "proper" principles, he joined others who opposed a national government founded on any principles, and together they attempted to weld a united opposition to ratification. The center of this activity was New York. George Clinton, governor of New York and a devout foe of nationalism, likewise was ready with articles denouncing the Constitution before it existed; and Clinton's printer, Thomas Greenleaf (publisher of the *New York Journal and Weekly Advertiser,* and printer to the state), printed and distributed Lee's five *Letters from the Federal Farmer* as a pamphlet, as he did the writings of many other anti-Federalists.

Lee's letters were dated October 8–15, 1787. The popularity of this pamphlet—it sold several thousand copies—as well as the momentum the Federalists were achieving, induced Lee to write a new series of essays. The new series, titled the same as the first, consisted of thirteen letters, dated from December 25, 1787, to January 25, 1788. It was not nearly so successful as the first, and it soon fell into obscurity.

In 1888, during the centennial celebrations of the ratification of the Constitution, Paul Leicester Ford published a book called *Pamphlets on the Constitution,* in which he republished Lee's first series of letters. He dismissed the thirteen additional letters as "largely repetitions of the first," and because Ford's book has for many years been the only easily available copy of Lee's work, the second series of letters all but disappeared from memory.

The present editor agrees with Ford's judgment in the main: letters 8–10, which are concerned largely with representation, letters 11 and 12, concerned with the Senate, letters 13 and 14, concerned with appointive offices, and letter 15, concerned with the judicial branch, are all not only repetitive of Lee's earlier arguments, but are also extremely verbose and tedious. Letters 6, 7, 16, and 17, on the other hand, are much more interesting, and they all bear directly on the central question in all these essays, balance in the federal system. For that reason these four of the second series are included in this collection.

The texts of both Dickinson's and Lee's *Letters* in the present edition are from first editions in the John Carter Brown Library, Brown University. The Dickinson text has been followed as closely as possible, even to the reproduction of errors. Thus, for example, Dickinson regularly misspelled the name of British statesman George Grenville, rendering it Greenville, and Dickinson's rendition has been followed here. In a few instances, however, absolute faithfulness to the original would yield absurd or misleading results, and minor modifications have been made. Dickinson's letters posed additional problems, for he followed the common pre-revolutionary practice of using a variety of typographical effects to achieve emphasis, and it has not always been possible to reproduce this convention with modern type. Inasmuch as no definitive edition of Lee's *Letters* exists—the eighteenth-century printings vary widely—the John Carter Brown Library edition has been standardized in terms of spelling, punctuation, and capitalization in order to make the substance more accessible to the modern reader.

Forrest McDonald

Letters from a Farmer in Pennsylvania

TO THE INHABITANTS OF THE BRITISH COLONIES

JOHN DICKINSON

LETTER I

My dear Countrymen,

I am a *Farmer*, settled, after a variety of fortunes, near the banks of the river *Delaware*, in the province of *Pennsylvania*. I received a liberal education, and have been engaged in the busy scenes of life; but am now convinced, that a man may be as happy without bustle, as with it. My farm is small; my servants are few, and good; I have a little money at interest; I wish for no more; my employment in my own affairs is easy; and with a contented grateful mind, undisturbed by worldly hopes or fears, relating to myself, I am completing the number of days allotted to me by divine goodness.

Being generally master of my time, I spend a good deal of it in a library, which I think the most valuable part of my small estate; and being acquainted with two or three gentlemen of abilities and learning, who honor me with their friendship, I have acquired, I believe, a greater knowledge in history, and the laws and constitution of my country, than is generally attained by men of my class, many of them not being so fortunate as I have been in the opportunities of getting information.

From my infancy I was taught to love *humanity* and *liberty*. Enquiry and experience have since confirmed my reverence for the lessons then given me, by convincing me more fully of their truth and excellence. Benevolence toward mankind, excites wishes for their welfare, and such wishes endear the means of fulfilling them. *These* can be found in liberty only, and therefore her sacred cause ought to be espoused by every man on every occasion, to the utmost of his power. As a charitable, but poor person does not withhold his *mite*, because he cannot relieve *all* the distresses of the miserable, so should not any honest man suppress his sentiments concerning freedom, however small their influence is likely to be. Perhaps he "may touch some wheel,"* that will have an effect greater than he could reasonably expect.

These being my sentiments, I am encouraged to offer to you, my countrymen, my thoughts on some late transactions, that appear to me to be of the utmost importance to you. Conscious of my own defects, I have waited some time, in expectation of seeing the subject treated by persons much better qualified for the task; but being therein disappointed, and apprehensive that longer delays will be injurious, I venture at length to request the attention of the public, praying, that these lines may be *read* with the same zeal for the happiness of *British America,* with which they were *wrote.*

With a good deal of surprise I have observed, that little notice has been taken of an act of parliament, as injurious in its principle to the liberties of these colonies, as the *Stamp Act* was: I mean the act for suspending the legislation of *New York.*

The assembly of that government complied with a former act of parliament, requiring certain provisions to be made for the troops in *America,* in every particular, I think, except the articles of salt, pepper and vinegar. In my opinion they acted imprudently, considering all circumstances, in not complying so far as would have given satisfaction, as several colonies did: But my dislike of their conduct in that instance, has not blinded me so much, that I cannot plainly perceive, that they have been punished in a manner pernicious to *American* freedom, and justly alarming to all the colonies.

If the *British* parliament has legal authority to issue an order, that we shall furnish a single article for the troops here, and to compel obedience to *that* order, they have the same right to issue an order for us to supply those troops with arms, clothes, and every necessary; and to compel obedience to *that* order also; in short, to lay *any burthens* they please upon us. What is this but *taxing* us at a *certain sum,* and leaving to us only the *manner* of raising it? How is this mode more tolerable than the *Stamp Act?* Would that act have appeared more pleasing to *Americans,* if being ordered thereby to raise the sum total of the taxes, the mighty privilege had been left to them, of saying

* Pope.

how much should be paid for an instrument of writing on paper, and how much for another on parchment?

An act of parliament, commanding us to do a certain thing, if it has any validity, is a *tax* upon us for the expense that accrues in complying with it; and for this reason, I believe, every colony on the continent, that chose to give a mark of their respect for *Great Britain,* in complying with the act relating to the troops, cautiously avoided the mention of that act, lest their conduct should be attributed to its supposed obligation.

The matter being thus stated, the assembly of *New York* either had, or had not, a right to refuse submission to that act. If they had, and I imagine no *American* will say they had not, then the parliament had *no right* to compel them to execute it. If they had not *this right,* they had *no right* to punish them for not executing it; and therefore *no right* to suspend their legislation, which is a punishment. In fact, if the people of *New York* cannot be legally taxed but by their own representatives, they cannot be legally deprived of the privilege of legislation, only for insisting on that exclusive privilege of taxation. If they may be legally deprived in such a case, of the privilege of legislation, why may they not, with equal reason, be deprived of every other privilege? Or why may not every colony be treated in the same manner, when any of them shall dare to deny their assent to any impositions, that shall be directed? Or what signifies the repeal of the *Stamp Act,* if these colonies are to lose their *other* privileges, by not tamely surrendering *that* of taxation?

There is one consideration arising from this suspension, which is not generally attended to, but shows its importance very clearly. It was not *necessary* that this suspension should be caused by an act of parliament. The crown might have restrained the governor of *New York,* even from calling the assembly together, by its prerogative in the royal governments. This step, I suppose, would have been taken, if the conduct of the assembly of *New York* had been regarded as an act of disobedience *to the crown alone;* but it is regarded as an act of "disobedience to the authority of the British Legislature."* This

* See the act of suspension.

gives the suspension a consequence vastly more affecting. It is a parliamentary assertion of the *supreme authority* of the *British* legislature over these colonies, in *the point of taxation*, and is intended to COMPEL *New York* into a submission to that authority. It seems therefore to me as much a violation of the liberties of the people of that province, and consequently of all these colonies, as if the parliament had sent a number of regiments to be quartered upon them till they should comply. For it is evident, that the suspension is meant as a *compulsion;* and the *method* of compelling is totally indifferent. It is indeed probable, that the sight of redcoats, and the hearing of drums, would have been most alarming; because people are generally more influenced by their eyes and ears, than by their reason. But whoever seriously considers the matter, must perceive that a dreadful stroke is aimed at the liberty of these colonies. I say, of these colonies; for the cause of *one* is the cause of *all.* If the parliament may lawfully deprive *New York* of any of *her* rights, it may deprive any, or all the other colonies of *their* rights; and nothing can possibly so much encourage such attempts, as a mutual inattention to the interests of each other. *To divide, and thus to destroy,* is the first political maxim in attacking those, who are powerful by their union. He certainly is not a wise man, who folds his arms, and reposes himself at home, viewing, with unconcern, the flames that have invaded his neighbor's house, without using any endeavors to extinguish them. When Mr. *Hampden's* ship money case, for *Three Shillings* and *Four-pence,* was tried, all the people of *England,* with anxious expectation, interested themselves in the important decision; and when the slightest point, touching the freedom of *one* colony, is agitated, I earnestly wish, that *all the rest* may, with equal ardor, support their sister. Very much may be said on this subject; but I hope, more at present is unnecessary.

With concern I have observed, that *two* assemblies of this province have sat and adjourned, without taking any notice of this act. It may perhaps be asked, what would have been proper for them to do? I am by no means fond of inflammatory measures; I detest them. I should be sorry that anything should be done which might justly displease our sovereign, or our mother country: But a firm, modest exertion of a free spirit, should never be wanting on public occasions.

It appears to me, that it would have been sufficient for the assembly to have ordered our agents to represent to the King's ministers their sense of the suspending act, and to pray for its repeal. Thus we should have borne our testimony against it; and might therefore reasonably expect that, on a like occasion, we might receive the same assistance from the other colonies.

Concordia res parvae crescunt.

Small things grow great by concord.

A Farmer
Nov. 5.*

LETTER II

My dear Countrymen,

There is another late act of parliament, which appears to me to be unconstitutional, and as destructive to the liberty of these colonies, as that mentioned in my last letter; that is, the act for granting the duties on paper, glass, etc.

The parliament unquestionably possesses a legal authority to *regulate* the trade of *Great Britain,* and all her colonies. Such an authority is essential to the relation between a mother country and her colonies; and necessary for the common good of all. He who considers these provinces as states distinct from the *British Empire,* has very slender notions of *justice,* or of their *interests.* We are but parts of a *whole;* and therefore there must exist a power somewhere, to preside, and preserve the connection in due order. This power is

* The day of King WILLIAM the Third's landing.

lodged in the parliament; and we are as much dependent on *Great Britain,* as a perfectly free people can be on another.

I have looked over *every statute* relating to these colonies, from their first settlement to this time; and I find every one of them founded on this principle, till the *Stamp Act* administration.* *All before,* are calculated to regulate trade, and preserve or promote a mutually

* For the satisfaction of the reader, recitals from the former acts of parliament relating to these colonies are added. By comparing these with the modern acts, he will perceive their great difference in *expression* and *intention.*

The 12th *Cha.* Chap. 18, which forms the foundation of the laws relating to *our* trade, by enacting that certain productions of the colonies should be carried to *England* only, and that no goods shall be imported from the plantations but in ships belonging to *England, Ireland, Wales, Berwick,* or the *Plantations,* etc. begins thus: "*For the increase of shipping,* and *encouragement of the navigation of this nation,* wherein, under the good providence and protection of GOD, the wealth, *safety,* and strength of this Kingdom is so much concerned," etc.

The 15th *Cha.* II. Chap. 7, enforcing the same regulation, assigns these reasons for it. "In regard his Majesty's plantations, beyond the seas, are inhabited and peopled by his subjects of this his Kingdom of *England; for the maintaining a greater correspondence and kindness between them,* and keeping them in a firmer dependence upon it, and rendering them yet more beneficial and advantageous unto it, *in the further employment and increase of* English *shipping and seamen, vent* of *English* woollen, and other manufacturers and commodities, *rendering the navigation to and from the same more safe and cheap,* and making this Kingdom a *staple,* not only of the commodities of those plantations, but also of the commodities of other countries and places *for the supplying of them;* and it being the *usage* of other nations to keep their plantations' trade to themselves," etc.

The 25th *Cha.* II, Chap. 7, made expressly "*for the better securing the plantation trade,*" which imposes duties on certain commodities exported from one colony to another, mentions this cause for imposing them: "Whereas by one act, passed in the 12th year of your Majesty's reign, intitled, An act for *encouragement of shipping and navigation,* and by several other laws, passed since that time, it is permitted to ship, etc. sugars, tobacco, etc. of the growth, etc. of any of your Majesty's plantations in *America,* etc. from the places of their growth, etc. to any other of your Majesty's plantations in those parts, etc. and that *without paying custom for the same,* either at the lading or unlading the said commodities, by means whereof the trade and navigation in those commodities, from one plantation to another, is greatly increased, and the inhabitants of divers of those colonies, *not contenting themselves with being supplied with those commodities for their own use, free from all customs* (while the subjects of this your kingdom of *England* have paid great customs and impositions for what of them hath been spent here) *but, contrary to the express letter of the aforesaid laws, have brought into divers parts of* Europe great quantities thereof, and do also vend great quantities thereof to the shipping of other nations, who bring them into divers parts of *Europe,* to the great hurt and diminution of your Majesty's customs, and of the *trade* and *navigation* of this your kingdom; FOR THE PREVENTION THEREOF, etc.

The 7th and 8th *Will.* III. Chap. 22, intitled, "An act for preventing frauds, and

beneficial intercourse between the several constituent parts of the empire; and though many of them imposed duties on trade, yet those duties were always imposed *with design* to restrain the commerce of one part, that was injurious to another, and thus to promote the general welfare. The raising of a revenue thereby was never intended. Thus the King, by his judges in his courts of justice, imposes fines, which all together amount to a very considerable sum, and contribute

---

regulating abuses in the plantation trade," recites that, "notwithstanding divers acts, etc. great abuses are daily committed, *to the prejudice of the* English *navigation, and the loss of a great part of the plantation trade* to this kingdom, by the *artifice* and *cunning* of ill disposed persons; FOR REMEDY WHEREOF, etc. And whereas in some of his Majesty's *American* plantations, a doubt or misconstruction has arisen upon the before mentioned act, made in the 25th year of the reign of King *Charles* II, whereby certain duties are laid upon the commodities therein enumerated (which by law may be transported from one plantation to another, for the supply of each other's wants) *as if* the same were, by the payment of those duties in one plantation, discharged from giving the securities intended by the aforesaid acts, made in the 12th, 22nd and 23rd years of the reign of King *Charles* II, and consequently be at liberty to go to any foreign market in *Europe*," etc.

The 6th *Anne*, Chap. 37, reciting the advancement of trade, and encouragement of ships of war, etc. grants to the captors the property of all prizes carried into *America*, subject to such customs and duties, as if the same had been first imported into any part of *Great Britain*, and from thence exported, etc.

This was a *gift to persons acting under commissions from the crown*, and therefore it was reasonable that the *terms* prescribed in that gift, should be complied with—more especially as the payment of such duties was intended to give a preference to the productions of *British* colonies, over those of other colonies. However, being found inconvenient to the colonies, about four years afterwards, this act was, *for that reason*, so far repealed, that by another act "all prize goods, imported into any part of *Great Britain*, from any of the plantations, were made liable to such duties only in *Great Britain*, as in case they had been of the growth and product of the plantations."

The 6th *Geo*. II Chap. 13, which imposes duties on foreign rum, sugar and molasses, imported into the colonies, *shews* the reasons thus—"Whereas the welfare and prosperity of your Majesty's sugar colonies in *America*, are of the greatest consequence and importance to the *trade*, *navigation*, and *strength* of this kingdom; and whereas the planters of the said sugar colonies, have of late years *fallen into such great discouragements*, that they are unable to improve or carry on the sugar trade *upon an equal footing* with the foreign sugar colonies, *without some advantage and relief be given to them from* Great Britain: FOR REMEDY WHEREOF, AND FOR THE GOOD AND WELFARE OF YOUR MAJESTY'S SUBJECTS," etc.

The 29th *Geo*. II Chap. 26, and the *1st Geo*. III Chap. 9, which continue the 6th *Geo*. II Chap. 13, declare, that the said act has, by experience, been found *useful* and *beneficial*, etc. These are all the most considerable statutes relating to the commerce of the colonies; and it is thought to be utterly unnecessary to add any observations to these extracts, to prove that they were all intended *solely as regulations of trade*.

to the support of government: But this is merely a consequence arising from restrictions that only meant to keep peace and prevent confusion; and surely a man would argue very loosely, who should conclude from hence, that the King has a right to levy money in general upon his subjects. Never did the *British* parliament, till the period above mentioned, think of imposing duties in *America* FOR THE PURPOSE OF RAISING A REVENUE. Mr. *Greenville* first introduced this language, in the preamble to the 4th of GEO. III Chap. 15, which has these words—"And whereas it is just and necessary that A REVENUE BE RAISED IN YOUR MAJESTY'S SAID DOMINIONS IN AMERICA, *for defraying the expenses of defending, protecting, and securing the same:* We your Majesty's most dutiful and loyal subjects, THE COMMONS OF GREAT BRITAIN, in parliament assembled, being desirous to make some provision in this present session of parliament, TOWARD RAISING THE SAID REVENUE IN AMERICA, have resolved to GIVE and GRANT unto your Majesty the several rates and duties herein after mentioned." etc.

A few months after came the *Stamp Act,* which reciting this, proceeds in the same strange mode of expression, thus—"And whereas it is just and necessary, that provision be made FOR RAISING A FURTHER REVENUE WITHIN YOUR MAJESTY'S DOMINIONS IN AMERICA, *towards defraying the said expences,* we your Majesty's most dutiful and loyal subjects, the COMMONS OF GREAT BRITAIN, etc. GIVE and GRANT," etc. as before.

The last act, granting duties upon paper, etc. carefully pursues these modern precedents. The preamble is, "Whereas it is expedient THAT A REVENUE SHOULD BE RAISED IN YOUR MAJESTY'S DOMINIONS IN AMERICA, *for making a more certain and adequate provision for defraying the charge of the administration of justice, and the support of civil government in such provinces, where it shall be found necessary; and towards further defraying the expences of defending, protecting and securing the said dominions, we your Majesty's most dutiful and loyal subjects,* the COMMONS OF GREAT BRITAIN, etc. GIVE and GRANT," etc. as before.

Here we may observe an authority *expressly* claimed and exerted to impose duties on these colonies; not for the regulation of trade; not for the preservation or promotion of a mutually beneficial intercourse between the several constituent parts of the empire, heretofore the *sole objects* of parliamentary institutions; *but for the single purpose of levying money upon us.*

This I call an innovation; and a most dangerous innovation.* It may perhaps be objected, that *Great Britain* has a right to lay what duties she pleases upon her exports,† and it makes no difference to us, whether they are paid here or there.

To this I answer. These colonies require many things for their use, which the laws of *Great Britain* prohibit them from getting any where but from her. Such are paper and glass.

That we may legally be bound to pay any *general* duties on these commodities, relative to the regulation of trade, is granted; but we being *obliged by her laws* to take them from *Great Britain,* any *special* duties imposed on their exportation *to us only, with intention to raise a revenue from us only,* are as much *taxes* upon us, as those imposed by the *Stamp Act.*

What is the difference in *substance* and *right,* whether the same sum is raised upon us by the rates mentioned in the *Stamp Act,* on the *use* of paper, or by these duties, on the *importation* of it. It is only the edition of a former book, shifting a sentence from the *end* to the *beginning.*

Suppose the duties were made payable in *Great Britain?*

It signifies nothing to us, whether they are to be paid here or there. Had the *Stamp Act* directed, that all the paper should be landed at *Florida,* and the duties paid there, before it was brought to the *British* colonies, would the act have raised less money upon us, or

* "It is worthy observation how quietly subsidies, granted in forms *usual* and *accustomable* (though heavy) are borne; such a power hath use and custom. On the other side, what discontentments and disturbances subsidies *framed in a new mold* do raise (SUCH AN INBRED HATRED NOVELTY DOTH HATCH) is evident by examples of former times." Lord *Coke's* 2nd Institute, p. 33.

† Some people think that *Great Britain* has the same right to impose duties on the exports to these colonies, as on the exports to *Spain* and *Portugal,* etc. Such persons attend so much to the idea of exportation, that they entirely drop *that of the connection between the mother country and her colonies.* If *Great Britain* had always claimed, and exercised an authority to compel *Spain* and *Portugal* to import manufactures from her only, the cases would be parallel: But as she never pretended to such a right, they are at liberty to get them where they please; and if they chuse to take them from her, rather than from other nations, they voluntarily consent to pay the duties imposed on them.

have been less destructive of our rights? By no means: For as we were under a necessity of using the paper, we should have been under the necessity of paying the duties. Thus, in the present case, a like *necessity* will subject us, if this act continues in force, to the payment of the duties now imposed.

Why was the *Stamp Act* then so pernicious to freedom? It did not enact, that every man in the colonies *should* buy a certain quantity of paper—No: It only directed, that no instrument of writing should be valid in law, if not made on stamped paper, etc.

The makers of that act knew full well, that the confusions that would arise from the disuse of writings, would COMPEL the colonies to use the stamped paper, and therefore to pay the taxes imposed. For this reason the *Stamp Act* was said to be a law THAT WOULD EXECUTE ITSELF. For the very same reason, the last act of parliament, if it is granted to have any force here, WILL EXECUTE ITSELF, and will be attended with the very same consequences to *American* liberty.

Some persons perhaps may say that this act lays us under no necessity to pay the duties imposed because we may ourselves manufacture the articles on which they are laid; whereas by the *Stamp Act* no instrument of writing could be good unless made on *British* paper, and that too stamped.

Such an objection amounts to no more than this, that the injury resulting to these colonies, from the total disuse of *British* paper and glass, will not be *so afflicting* as that which would have resulted from the total disuse of writing among them; for by that means even the *Stamp Act* might have been eluded. Why then was it universally detested by them as slavery itself? Because it presented to these devoted provinces nothing but a choice of calamities,* embittered by indignities, each of which it was unworthy of free men to bear. But is no injury a violation of right but the *greatest* injury? If the eluding the payment of the taxes imposed by the *Stamp Act,* would have subjected us to a more dreadful inconvenience than the eluding of the payment of those imposed by the late act; does it therefore follow,

* Either the *disuse* of writing, or the payment of *taxes* imposed by others *without our consent.*

that the last is *no violation* of our rights, tho' it is calculated for the same purpose the other was, that is, to *raise money upon us,* WITHOUT OUR CONSENT?

This would be making *right* to consist, not in an exemption from *injury,* but from a certain *degree of injury.*

But the objectors may further say, that we shall suffer no injury at all by the disuse of *British* paper and glass. We might not, if we could make as much as we want. But can any man, acquainted with *America,* believe this possible? I am told there are but two or three *Glass-Houses* on this continent, and but very few *Paper-Mills;* and suppose more should be erected, a long course of years must elapse, before they can be brought to perfection. This continent is a country of planters, farmers, and fishermen; not of manufactures. The difficulty of establishing particular manufactures in such a country, is almost insufferable. For one manufacture is connected with others in such a manner, that it may be said to be impossible to establish one or two without establishing several others. The experience of many nations may convince us of this truth.

Inexpressible therefore must be our distresses in evading the late acts, by the disuse of *British* paper and glass. Nor will this be the extent of our misfortune, if we admit the legality of that act.

Great Britain has prohibited the manufacturing *iron* and *steel* in these colonies, without any objection being made to her *right* of doing it. The *like* right she must have to prohibit any other manufacture among us. Thus she is possessed of an undisputed *precedent* on that point. This authority, she will say, is founded on the *original intention* of settling these colonies; that is, that she should manufacture for them, and that they should supply her with materials. The *equity* of this policy, she will also say, has been universally acknowledged by the colonies, who never have made the least objection to statutes for that purpose; and will further appear by the *mutual benefits* flowing from this usage, ever since the settlement of these colonies.

Our great advocate, Mr. *Pitt,* in his speeches on the debate concerning the repeal of the *Stamp Act,* acknowledged, that *Great Britain* could restrain our manufactures. His words are these—"This kingdom, as the supreme governing and legislative power, has ALWAYS bound the colonies by her regulations and RESTRICTIONS in trade, in navigation, in MANUFACTURES—in everything, *except that of taking their money out of their pockets* WITHOUT THEIR CONSENT." Again he says, "We may bind their trade, CONFINE THEIR MANUFACTURES, and exercise every power whatever, *except that of taking their money out of their pockets* WITHOUT THEIR CONSENT."

Here then, my dear countrymen, ROUSE yourselves, and behold the ruin hanging over your heads. If you ONCE admit, that *Great Britain* may lay duties upon her exportations to us, *for the purpose of levying money on us only,* she then will have nothing to do, but to lay those duties on the articles which she prohibits us to manufacture—and the tragedy of *American* liberty is finished. We have been prohibited from procuring manufactures, in all cases, any where but from *Great Britain* (excepting linens, which we are permitted to import directly from *Ireland*). We have been prohibited, in some cases, from manufacturing for ourselves; and may be prohibited in others. We are therefore exactly in the situation of a city besieged, which is surrounded by the works of the besiegers in every part *but one.* If *that* is closed up, no step can be taken, *but to surrender at discretion.* If *Great Britain* can order us to come to her for necessaries we want, and can order us to pay what taxes she pleases before we take them away, or when we land them here, we are as abject slaves as *France* and *Poland* can show in wooden shoes and with uncombed hair.*

Perhaps the nature of the *necessities* of dependent states, caused by the policy of a governing one for her own benefit, may be elucidated by a fact mentioned in history. When the *Carthaginians* were possessed of the island of *Sardinia,* they made a decree, that the *Sardinians* should not raise corn, nor get it any other way than from the Carthaginians. Then, by imposing any duties they would upon it, they drained from the miserable Sardinians any sums they pleased; and whenever that oppressed people made the least movement to assert their liberty, their tyrant starved them to death or submission. This may be called the most perfect kind of political necessity.

* The peasants of *France* wear wooden shoes; and the vassals of *Poland* are remarkable for matted hair which never can be combed.

From what has been said, I think this uncontrovertible conclusion may be deduced, that when a ruling state obliges a dependent state to take certain commodities from her alone, it is implied in the nature of that obligation; is essentially requisite to give it the least degree of justice; and is inseparably united with it, in order to preserve any share of freedom to the dependent state; *that those commodities should never be loaded with duties,* FOR THE SOLE PURPOSE OF LEVYING MONEY ON THE DEPENDENT STATE.

Upon the whole, the single question is, whether the parliament can legally impose duties to be paid *by the people of these colonies only,* FOR THE SOLE PURPOSE OF RAISING A REVENUE, *on commodities which she obliges us to take from her alone,* or, in other words, whether the parliament can legally take money out of our pockets, without our consent. If they can, our boasted liberty is but

Vox et praeterea nihil.

A sound and nothing else.

A Farmer

LETTER III

My dear Countrymen,

I rejoice to find that my two former letters to you have been generally received with so much favor by such of you, whose sentiments I have had an opportunity of knowing. Could you look into my heart you would instantly perceive a zealous attachment to your interests, and a lively resentment of every insult and injury offered to you, to be the motives that have engaged me to address you.

I am no further concerned in anything affecting *America,* than any one of you; and when liberty leaves it, I can quit it much more conveniently than most of you: But while Divine Providence, that gave me existence in a land of freedom, permits my head to think, my lips to speak, and my hand to move, I shall so highly and gratefully value the blessing received as to take care that my silence and inactivity shall not give my implied assent to any act, degrading my brethren and myself from the birthright, wherewith heaven itself "*hath made us free.*"*

Sorry I am to learn that there are some few persons who shake their heads with solemn motion, and pretend to wonder, what can be the meaning of these letters. "*Great Britain,*" they say, "is too powerful to contend with; she is determined to oppress us; it is in vain to speak of right on one side, when there is power on the other; when we are strong enough to resist we shall attempt it; but now we are not strong enough, and therefore we had better be quiet; it signifies nothing to convince us that our rights are invaded when we cannot defend them; and if we should get into riots and tumults about the late act, it will only draw down heavier displeasure upon us."

What can such men design? What do their grave observations amount to, but this—"that these colonies, totally regardless of their liberties, should commit them, with humble resignation, to *chance, time,* and the tender mercies of *ministers.*"

Are these men ignorant that usurpations, which might have been successfully opposed at first, acquire strength by continuance, and thus become irresistible? Do they condemn the conduct of these colonies, concerning the *Stamp Act?* Or have they forgot its successful issue? Should the colonies at that time, instead of acting as they did, have trusted for relief to the fortuitous events of futurity? If it is needless "to speak of rights" now, it was as needless then. If the behavior of the colonies was prudent and glorious then, and successful too; it will be equally prudent and glorious to act in the same manner now, if our rights *are* equally invaded, and may be as successful. Therefore it becomes necessary to inquire whether "our rights are invaded." To talk of "defending" them, as if they could be no otherwise

* Galatians 5:1.

"defended" than by arms, is as much out of the way, as if a man having a choice of several roads to reach his journey's end, should prefer the worst, for no other reason, but because it *is* the worst.

As to "riots and tumults," the gentlemen who are so apprehensive of them, are much mistaken, if they think that grievances cannot be redressed without such assistance.

I will now tell the gentlemen, what is "the meaning of these letters." The meaning of them is, to convince the people of these colonies that they are at this moment exposed to the most imminent dangers; and to persuade them immediately, vigorously, and unanimously, to exert themselves in the most firm, but most peaceable manner, for obtaining relief.

The cause of *liberty* is a cause of too much dignity to be sullied by turbulence and tumult. It ought to be maintained in a manner suitable to her nature. Those who engage in it, should breathe a sedate, yet fervent spirit, animating them to actions of prudence, justice, modesty, bravery, humanity and magnanimity.

To such a wonderful degree were the ancient *Spartans,* as brave and free a people as ever existed, inspired by this happy temperature of soul, that rejecting even in their battles the use of trumpets and other instruments for exciting heat and rage, they marched up to scenes of havoc, and horror,* with the sound of flutes, to the tunes of which their steps kept pace—"exhibiting," as *Plutarch* says, "at once a terrible and delightful fight, and proceeding with a deliberate valor, full of hope and good assurance, as if some divinity had sensibly assisted them."

I hope, my dear countrymen, that you will, in every colony, be upon your guard against those who may at any time endeavor to stir you up, under pretenses of patriotism, to any measures disrespectful to our Sovereign, and our mother country. Hot, rash, disorderly proceedings, injure the reputation of the people as to wisdom, valor, and virtue, without procuring them the least benefit. I pray GOD that he may be pleased to inspire you and your posterity, to the latest ages, with a spirit of which I have an idea, that I find a difficulty to

* *Plutarch* in the life of *Lycurgus.* Archbishop Potter's "*Archaeologia Graeca.*"

express. To express it in the best manner I can, I mean a spirit that shall so guide you that it will be impossible to determine whether an *American's* character is most distinguishable for his loyalty to his Sovereign, his duty to his mother country, his love of freedom, or his affection for his native soil.

Every government at some time or other falls into wrong measures. These may proceed from mistake or passion. But every such measure does not dissolve the obligation between the governors and the governed. The mistake may be corrected; the passion may subside. It is the duty of the governed to endeavor to rectify the mistake, and to appease the passion. They have not at first any other right, than to represent their grievances, and to pray for redress, unless an emergency is so pressing as not to allow time for receiving an answer to their applications, which rarely happens. If their applications are disregarded, then that kind of *opposition* becomes justifiable which can be made without breaking the laws or disturbing the public peace. This conflicts in the *prevention of the oppressors reaping advantage from their oppressions,* and not in their punishment. For experience may teach them what reason did not; and harsh methods cannot be proper until milder ones have failed.

If at length it becomes UNDOUBTED that an inveterate resolution is formed to annihilate the liberties of the governed, the *English* history affords frequent examples of resistance by force. What particular circumstances will in any future case justify such resistance can never be ascertained till they happen. Perhaps it may be allowable to say generally, that it never can be justifiable until the people are FULLY CONVINCED that any further submission will be destructive to their happiness.

When the appeal is made to the sword, highly probable is it, that the punishment will exceed the offense; and the calamities attending on war outweigh those preceding it. These considerations of justice and prudence, will always have great influence with good and wise men.

To these reflections on this subject, it remains to be added, and ought for ever to be remembered, that resistance, in the case of colonies against their mother country, is extremely different from the resistance of a people against their prince. A nation may change their king, or race of kings, and, retaining their ancient form of government, be gainers by changing. Thus *Great Britain,* under the illustrious house of *Brunswick,* a house that seems to flourish for the happiness of mankind, has found a felicity unknown in the reigns of the *Stuarts.* But if once *we* are separated from our mother country, what new form of government shall we adopt, or where shall we find another *Britain* to supply our loss? Torn from the body, to which we are united by religion, liberty, laws, affections, relation, language and commerce, we must bleed at every vein.

In truth—the prosperity of these provinces is founded in their dependence on *Great Britain;* and when she returns to her "old good humor, and her old good nature," as Lord *Clarendon* expresses it, I hope they will always think it their duty and interest, as it most certainly will be, to promote her welfare by all the means in their power.

We cannot act with too much caution in our disputes. Anger produces anger; and differences, that might be accommodated by kind and respectful behavior, may, by imprudence, be enlarged to an incurable rage. In quarrels between countries, as well as in those between individuals, when they have risen to a certain height, the first cause of dissension is no longer remembered, the minds of the parties being wholly engaged in recollecting and resenting the mutual expressions of their dislike. When feuds have reached that fatal point, all considerations of reason and equity vanish; and a blind fury governs, or rather confounds all things. A people no longer regards their interest, but the gratification of their wrath. The sway of the *Cleons and Clodiuses,** the designing and detectable flatterers of the *prevailing passion,* becomes confirmed. Wise and good men in vain oppose the storm, and may think themselves fortunate, if, in attempting to preserve their ungrateful fellow citizens, they do not ruin themselves. Their *prudence* will be called *baseness;* their *moderation* will be called guilt; and if their virtue does not lead them to destruction, as that

* *Cleon* was a popular firebrand of *Athens,* and *Clodius* of *Rome;* each of whom plunged his country into the deepest calamities.

of many other great and excellent persons has done, they may survive to receive from their expiring country the mournful glory of her acknowledgment, that their counsels, if regarded, would have saved her.

The constitutional modes of obtaining relief are those which I wish to see pursued on the present occasion; that is, by petitions of our assemblies, or where they are not permitted to meet, of the people, to the powers that can afford us relief.

We have an excellent prince, in whose good dispositions toward us we may confide. We have a generous, sensible and humane nation, to whom we may apply. They may be deceived. They may, by artful men, be provoked to anger against us. I cannot believe they will be cruel and unjust; or that their anger will be implacable. Let us behave like dutiful children who have received unmerited blows from a beloved parent. Let us complain to our parent; but let our complaints speak at the same time the language of affliction and veneration.

If, however, it shall happen, by an unfortunate course of affairs, that our applications to his Majesty and the parliament for redress, prove ineffectual, let us then take *another step*, by withholding from *Great Britain* all the advantages she has been used to receive from us. Then let us try, if our ingenuity, industry, and frugality, will not give weight to our remonstrances. Let us all be united with one spirit, in one cause. Let us invent—let us work—let us save—let us, continually, keep up our claim, and incessantly repeat our complaints—But, above all, let us implore the protection of that infinitely good and gracious being, "by whom kings reign, and princes decree justice."*

Nil desperandum.

Nothing is to be despaired of.

A Farmer

* Proverbs 8:15.

LETTER IV

My dear Countrymen,

An objection, I hear, has been made against my second letter, which I would willingly clear up before I proceed. "There is," say these objectors, "a material difference between the *Stamp Act* and the *late act* for laying a duty on paper, etc. that justifies the conduct of those who opposed the former, and yet are willing to submit to the latter. The duties imposed by the *Stamp Act* were *internal* taxes; but the present are *external,* and therefore the parliament may have a right to impose them."

To this I answer, with a total denial of the power of parliament to lay upon these colonies any "*tax*" whatever.

This point, being so important to this, and to succeeding generations, I wish to be clearly understood.

To the word "*tax,*" I annex that meaning which the constitution and history of *England* require to be annexed to it; that is—that it is *an imposition on the subject, for the sole purpose of levying money.*

In the early ages of our monarchy, certain services were rendered to the crown *for the general good.* These were personal:* But in process

* It is very worthy of remark, how watchful our wise ancestors were, lest their *services* should be increased beyond what the law allowed. No man was bound to go out of the realm to serve the King. Therefore, even in the conquering reign of *Henry the Fifth,* when the martial spirit of the nation was highly inflamed by the heroic courage of their Prince, and by his great success, they still carefully guarded against the establishment of illegal services. "When this point (says Lord Chief Justice *Coke*) concerning maintenance of wars out of *England,* came in question, the COMMONS did make their *continual claim* of their *ancient freedom* and *birthright,* as in the first of *Henry the Fifth,* and in the seventh of *Henry the Fifth,* etc. the COMMONS made a PROTEST, that they were not bound to the maintenance of war in *Scotland, Ireland, Calice, France, Normandy,* or other *foreign* parts, and caused their PROTESTS to be entered into the parliament rolls, where they yet remain; which, in effect, agrees with that which, upon like occasion, was made in the parliament of the 15th *Edward* I." (2d Inst. p. 528)

of time, such institutions being found inconvenient, gifts and grants of their own property were made by the people, under the several names of aids, tallages, talks, taxes and subsidies, etc. These were made, as may be collected even from the names, for public service upon "need and necessity."* All these sums were levied upon the people by virtue of their voluntary gift.† Their intention was to support the *national honor and interest.* Some of those grants comprehended duties arising from trade; being imports on merchandizes. These Lord Chief Justice *Coke* classes under "subsidies," and "parliamentary aids." They are also called "customs." But whatever the name was, they were always considered as *gifts of the people to the crown, to be employed for public uses.*

Commerce was at a low ebb, and surprising instances might be produced how little it was attended to for a succession of ages. The terms that have been mentioned, and, among the rest, that of "tax," had obtained a national, parliamentary meaning, drawn from the principles of the constitution, long before any *Englishman* thought of *imposition of duties, for the regulation of trade.*

* 4th Inst. p. 28.

† *Reges Angliae, nihil tale, nisi convocatis primis ordinibus, et assentiente populo suscipiunt.* (Phil. Comines. 2d *Inst*)

These gifts entirely depending on the pleasure of the donors, were proportioned to the abilities of the several ranks of people who gave, and were regulated by *their* opinion of the public necessities. Thus *Edward* I had in his 11th year a *thirtieth* from the *laity,* a *twentieth* from the *clergy;* in his 22nd year a TENTH from the *laity,* a *sixth* from *London,* and other corporate towns, *half of their benefices* from the *clergy;* in his 23d year an *eleventh* from the *barons* and others, a *tenth* from the *clergy;* a *seventh* from the *burgesses,* etc. (*Hume's Hist. of England*)

The same difference in the grants of the several ranks is observable in other reigns.

In the famous statute *de tallagio non concedendo,* the king enumerates the several *classes,* without whose consent, he and his heirs never should set or levy any tax—"*nullum tallagium, vel auxilium per nos, vel beredes nostros in regno nestro ponatur feu levetur, sine voluntate et assenfu archiepiscoporum, episcoporum, comitum, baronum, militum, burgensium, et aliorum liberorum com. de regno nostro.*" (34th *Edward* I)

Lord Chief Justice *Coke,* in his comment on these words, says—"for the quieting of the *commons,* and for a *perpetual and constant law for ever after,* both in this AND OTHER LIKE CASES, this act was made." These words are "*plain,* WITHOUT ANY SCRUPLE, *absolute,* WITHOUT ANY SAVING." 2d *Coke's Inst.* p. 532, 533. Little did the venerable judge imagine, that "*other* LIKE *cases*" would happen, in which the spirit of this law would be despised by *Englishmen,* the posterity of those who made it.

Whenever we speak of "taxes" among *Englishmen,* let us therefore speak of them with reference to the *principles* on which, and the *intentions* with which they have been established. This will give certainty to our expression, and safety to our conduct: But if, when we have in view the liberty of these colonies, we proceed in any other course, we pursue a JUNO* indeed, but shall only catch a cloud.

In the national, parliamentary sense insisted on, the word "tax"† was certainly understood by the congress at New York, whose resolves may be said to form the *American* "bill of rights."

The third, fourth, fifth, and sixth resolves, are thus expressed.

III. "That it is *inseparably essential to the freedom of a people, and the undoubted right of Englishmen,* that NO TAX‡ be imposed on them, *except with their own consent,* given personally, or by their representatives."

IV. "That the people of the colonies are not, and from their local circumstances, cannot be represented in the house of commons in *Great Britain.*"

V. "That the only representatives of the people of the colonies, are the persons chosen therein by themselves; and that NO TAXES ever have been, or can be constitutionally imposed on them, but by their respective legislatures."

VI. "That ALL *supplies to the crown,* being free gifts of the people, it is *unreasonable, and inconsistent with the principles and spirit of the* British *constitution,* for the people of *Great Britain* to grant to his Majesty *the property of the colonies.*"

Here is no distinction made between *internal* and *external* taxes. It is evident from the short reasoning thrown into these resolves, that every imposition "to grant to his Majesty *the property of the colonies,*" was thought a "tax"; and that every such imposition, if laid any other way, than "with their consent, given personally, or by their

* The Goddess of *Empire,* in the Heathen Mythology; according to an ancient fable, *Ixion* pursued her, but she escaped in a cloud.

† In this sense *Montesquieu* uses the word "tax," in his 13th book of *Spirit of Laws.*

‡ The rough draft of the resolves of the congress at *New York* are now in my hands, and from some notes on that draft, and other particular reasons, I am satisfied, that the congress understood the word "tax" in the sense here contended for.

representatives," was not only "unreasonable, and inconsistent with the principles and spirit of the *British* constitution," but destructive "to the freedom of a people."

This language is clear and important. A "TAX" means an imposition to raise money. Such persons therefore as speak of *internal* and *external* "TAXES," I pray may pardon me, if I object to that expression, as applied to the privileges and interests of these colonies. There may be *internal* and *external* IMPOSITIONS, founded on *different principles,* and having *different tendencies;* every "tax" being an imposition, though every imposition is not a "tax." But *all taxes* are founded on the *same principle;* and have the *same tendency.*

External impositions, for the regulation of our trade, do not "grant to his Majesty *the property of the colonies.*" They only *prevent the colonies acquiring property,* in things not necessary, in a manner judged to be injurious to the welfare of the whole empire. But the last statute respecting us, "grants to his Majesty *the property of the colonies,*" by laying duties on the manufactures of *Great Britain* which they MUST take, and which she settled them, on purpose that they SHOULD take.

WHAT *tax* can be more *internal* than this?* Here is money drawn,

* It seems to be evident, that Mr. *Pitt,* in his defense of *America,* during the debate concerning the repeal of the *Stamp Act,* by "*internal* taxes," meant any duties "for the purpose of raising a revenue"; and by "*external* taxes," meant duties imposed "for the regulation of trade." His expressions are these—"If the gentleman does not understand the differences between *internal* and *external* taxes, I cannot help it; but there is a plain distinction between taxes levied FOR THE PURPOSES OF RAISING A REVENUE, and duties imposed FOR THE REGULATION OF TRADE, for the accommodation of the subject; although, in the consequences, some revenue might incidentally arise from the latter."

These words were in Mr. *Pitt's* reply to Mr. *Greenville,* who said he could not understand the difference between external and internal taxes.

In every other part of his speeches on that occasion, his words confirm this construction of his expressions. The following extracts will show how positive and general were his assertions of our right.

"It is my opinion that this Kingdom has NO RIGHT to lay A TAX upon the colonies"—"The *Americans* are the SONS, not the BASTARDS of *England.* TAXATION is NO PART of the *governing* or *legislative* power"—"The *taxes* are a voluntary *gift* and *grant* of the *commons* ALONE. In LEGISLATION the THREE estates of the realm are ALIKE concerned, but the concurrence of the PEERS and the CROWN to a TAX, is only necessary to close with the FORM of a law.

The GIFT and GRANT is of the COMMONS ALONE"—"*The distinction between* LEGISLA-

without their consent, from a society, who have constantly enjoyed a constitutional mode of raising all money among themselves. The payment of this *tax* they have no possible method of avoiding; as they cannot do without the commodities on which it is laid, and they cannot manufacture these commodities themselves. Besides, if this unhappy country should be so lucky as to elude this act, by getting parchment enough, in the place of paper, or by reviving the ancient method of writing on wax and bark, and by inventing something to serve instead of glass, her ingenuity would stand her in little stead; for then the parliament would have nothing to do but to prohibit such manufactures, or to lay a tax on *hats* and WOOLEN CLOTHS, which they have already prohibited the colonies *from supplying each other with;* or on instruments and tools of *steel* and *iron,* which they have prohibited the provincials *from manufacturing at all:** And then, what little gold and silver they have, must be torn from their hands,

TION and TAXATION *is essentially necessary to liberty*"—"The COMMONS of *America,* represented in their several assemblies, have ever been in possession of the exercise of this their constitutional right, of GIVING and GRANTING their OWN MONEY. *They would have been* SLAVES, *if they had not enjoyed it.*" "The idea of a *virtual* representation of *America* in this house, is the most contemptible idea that ever entered into the head of man—It does not deserve a serious refutation."

He afterwards shows the unreasonableness of *Great Britain* taxing *America,* thus—"When I had the honor of serving his Majesty, I availed myself of the means of information, which I derived from my office, I SPEAK THEREFORE FROM KNOWLEDGE. My materials were good. I was at pains to *collect,* to *digest,* to *consider* them; and *I will be bold to affirm,* that the profit to *Great Britain* from the trade of the colonies, through all its branches, is TWO MILLIONS A YEAR. *This* is the fund that carried you triumphantly through the last war. The estates that were rented at two thousand pounds a year, threescore years ago, are three thousand pounds at present. Those estates sold then from fifteen to eighteen years purchase; the same may now be sold for thirty. YOU OWE THIS TO AMERICA. THIS IS THE PRICE THAT AMERICA PAYS YOU FOR HER PROTECTION"—"I dare not say how much higher these profits may be augmented"—"Upon the whole, I will beg leave to tell the house what is really my opinion; it is, that the *Stamp Act* be repealed absolutely, totally, and immediately. That the reason for the repeal be assigned, because it was founded on an ERRONEOUS PRINCIPLE."

* "And that pig and bar iron, made in his Majesty's colonies in America, may be further manufactured in this kingdom, be it further enacted by the authority aforesaid, that from and after the twenty-fourth day of June, 1750, no mill, or other engine, for slitting or rolling of iron, or any plating forge, to work with a tilt hammer, or any furnace for making steel, shall be erected; or, after such erection, continued in any of his Majesty's colonies in America." 23d *Geo.* II. Chap. 29, Sect. 9.

or they will not be able, in a short time, to get an ax* for cutting their firewood, nor a plough for raising their food. In what respect, therefore, I beg leave to ask, is the late act preferable to the *Stamp Act,* or more consistent with the liberties of the colonies? For my own part, I regard them both with equal apprehension; and think they ought to be in the same manner opposed.

> *Habemus quidem senatus consultum, tanquam gladium in vagina repositum.*
>
> We have a statute, laid up for future use, like a sword in the scabbard.

A Farmer

LETTER V

My dear Countrymen,

Perhaps the objection to the late act, imposing duties upon paper, etc. might have been safely rested on the argument drawn from the universal conduct of parliaments and ministers, from the first existence of these colonies, to the administration of Mr. *Greenville.*

What but the indisputable, the acknowledged exclusive right of the colonies to tax themselves, could be the reason, that in this long period of more than one hundred and fifty years, no statute was ever passed for the sole purpose of raising a revenue on the colonies? And how clear, how cogent must that reason be, to which every parliament,

* Though these particulars are mentioned as being absolutely necessary, yet perhaps they are not more so than glass in our severe winters, to keep out the cold from our houses; or than paper, without which such inexpressible confusions must ensue.

and every minister, for so long a time submitted, without a single attempt to innovate?

England, in part of that course of years, and *Great Britain,* in other parts, was engaged in several fierce and expensive wars; troubled with some tumultuous and bold parliaments; governed by many daring and wicked ministers; yet none of them ever ventured to touch the *Palladium* of *American* liberty. Ambition, avarice, faction, tyranny, all revered it. Whenever it was necessary to raise money on the colonies, the requisitions of the crown were made, and dutifully complied with. The parliament, from time to time, regulated their trade, and that of the rest of the empire, to preserve their dependence, and the connection of the whole in good order.

The people of *Great Britain,* in support of their privileges, boast much of their antiquity. It is true they are ancient; yet it may well be questioned, if there is a single privilege of a *British* subject, supported by longer, more solemn, or more uninterrupted testimony, than the exclusive right of taxation in these colonies. The people of *Great Britain* consider that kingdom as the sovereign of these colonies, and would now annex to that sovereignty a prerogative never heard of before. How would they bear this, was the case their own? What would they think of a *new* prerogative claimed by the crown? We may guess what their conduct would be, from the transports of passion into which they fell about the late embargo, tho' laid to relieve the most emergent necessities of state, admitting of no delay; and for which there were numerous precedents. Let our liberties be treated with the same tenderness and it is all we desire.

Explicit as the conduct of parliaments, for so many ages, is, to prove that no money can be levied on these colonies by parliament, for the purpose of raising a revenue, yet it is not the only evidence in our favor.

Every one of the most material arguments against the legality of the *Stamp Act,* operates with equal force against the act now objected to; but as they are well known, it seems unnecessary to repeat them here.

This general one only shall be considered at present: That tho' these colonies are dependent on *Great Britain;* and tho' she has a legal power to make laws for preserving that dependence; yet it is not necessary for this purpose, nor essential to the relation between a mother country and her colonies, as was eagerly contended by the advocates for the *Stamp Act,* that she should raise money on them without their consent.

Colonies were formerly planted by warlike nations, to keep their enemies in awe; to relieve their country, overburdened with inhabitants; or to discharge a number of discontented and troublesome citizens. But in more modern ages, the spirit of violence being, in some measure, if the expression may be allowed, sheathed in commerce, colonies have been settled by the nations of *Europe* for the purposes of trade. These purposes were to be attained, by the colonies raising for their mother country those things which she did not produce herself; and by supplying themselves from her with things they wanted. These were the *national objects* in the commencement of our colonies, and have been uniformly so in their promotion.

To answer these grand purposes, perfect liberty was known to be necessary; all history proving, that trade and freedom are nearly related to each other. By a due regard to this wise and just plan, the infant colonies, exposed in the unknown climates and unexplored wildernesses of this new world, lived, grew, and flourished.

The parent country, with undeviating prudence and virtue, attentive to the first principles of colonization, drew to herself the benefits she might reasonably expect, and preserved to her children the blessings on which those benefits were founded. She made laws, obliging her colonies to carry to her all those products which she wanted for her own use; and all those raw materials which she chose herself to work up. Besides this restriction, she forbade them to procure *manufactures* from any other part of the globe, or even the *products* of *European* countries, which alone could rival her, without being first brought to her. In short, by a variety of laws, she regulated their trade in such a manner as she thought most conducive to their mutual advantage, and her own welfare. A power was reserved to the crown of *repealing* any laws that should be enacted: The *executive* authority of government was also lodged in the crown, and its representatives; and an *appeal* was secured to the crown from all judgments in the administration of justice.

For all these powers, established by the mother country over the colonies; for all these immense emoluments derived by her from them; for all their difficulties and distresses in fixing themselves, what was the recompense made them? A communication of her rights in general, and particularly of that great one, the foundation of all the rest—that their property, acquired with so much pain and hazard, should be disposed of by none but themselves*—or, to use the beautiful and emphatic language of the sacred scriptures,† "that they should sit *every man* under his vine, and under his fig-tree, and NONE SHOULD MAKE THEM AFRAID."

Can any man of candor and knowledge deny, that these institutions form an affinity between *Great Britain* and her colonies, that sufficiently secures their dependence upon her? Or that for her to levy taxes upon them, is to reverse the nature of things? Or that she can pursue such a measure, without reducing them to a state of vassalage?

If any person cannot conceive the supremacy of *Great Britain* to exist, without the power of laying taxes to levy money upon us, the history of the colonies, and of *Great Britain,* since their settlement, will prove the contrary. He will there find the amazing advantages arising to her from them—the constant exercise of her supremacy—and their filial submission to it, without a single rebellion, or even the thought of one, from their first emigration to this moment—And all these things have happened, without one instance of *Great Britain's* laying taxes to levy money upon them.

How many *British*‡ *authors* have demonstrated that the present

* "The power of *taxing themselves,* was the privilege of which the *English* were, with reason, *particularly jealous.*" (Hume's *Hist. of England*)

† Mic. iv. 4.

‡ It has been said in the House of Commons, when complaints have been made of the decay of trade to any part of *Europe,* "That such things were not worth regard, as *Great Britain* was possessed of colonies that could consume more of her manufactures than she was able to supply them with." "As the case now stands, we shall show that the plantations are a spring of *wealth* to this nation, that they work for us, that their

wealth, power and glory of their country, are founded upon these colonies? As constantly as streams tend to the ocean, have they been pouring the fruits of all their labors into their mother's lap. Good heaven! and shall a total oblivion of former tendernesses and blessings, be spread over the minds of a good and wise nation, by the sordid arts of intriguing men, who, covering their selfish projects under

---

TREASURE CENTERS ALL HERE, and that the laws have tied them fast enough to us; so that it must be through our own fault and mismanagement, if they become independent of *England.*" (Davenant *on the Plantation Trade*)

"It is better that the islands should be supplied from the Northern Colonies than from *England;* for this reason, the provisions we might send to *Barbados, Jamaica,* etc. would be *unimproved* product of the earth, as grain of all kinds, or such product where there is little got by the improvement, as malt, salt beef and pork; indeed the exportation of salt first thither would be more advantageous, but the goods which we send to the *Northern Colonies,* are such, whose *improvement* may be justly said, one with another, to be near *four fifths* of the value of the *whole commodity,* as apparel, household furniture, and many other things." (*Idem*)

"*New England* is the most prejudicial plantation to the kingdom of *England;* and yet, to do right to that most industrious *English* colony, I must confess, that though we lose by their unlimited trade with other foreign plantations, yet we are very great gainers by their direct trade to and from *Old England.* Our yearly exportations of *English* manufactures, malt and other goods, from hence thither, amounting, in my opinion, to *ten times* the value of what is imported from there; which calculation I do not make at random, but upon *mature consideration,* and, peradventure, upon *as much experience in this very trade,* as any other person will pretend to; and therefore, whenever reformation of our correspondency in trade with that people shall be thought on, it will, in my poor judgment, require GREAT TENDERNESS, and VERY SERIOUS CIRCUMSPECTION." (Sir Josiah Child's *Discourse on Trade*)

"Our plantations spend mostly our *English* manufactures, and those *of all sorts almost imaginable,* in *egregious quantities,* and employ nearly *two thirds of all our* English *shipping; so that we have more people* in *England,* by reason of our plantations in *America.*" (*Idem*)

Sir Josiah Child says, in another part of his work, "That not more than fifty families are maintained in *England* by the refining of sugar." From whence, and from what *Davenant* says, it is plain, that the advantages here said to be derived from the plantations by *England,* must be meant chiefly of the continental colonies.

"I shall sum up my whole remarks in our *American* colonies, with this observation, that as they are a certain annual revenue of SEVERAL MILLIONS STERLING to their mother country, they ought carefully to be protected, duly encouraged, and at every opportunity that presents itself, improved for their increment and advantage, as every one they can possibly reap, must at last return to us with interest." (BEAWES'S Lex Merc. Red.)

"We may safely advance, that our trade and navigation are greatly increased by our colonies, and that they really are a source of treasure and naval power to this kingdom, since THEY WORK FOR US, AND THEIR TREASURE CENTERS HERE. Before their settlement, our manufactures were few, and those but indifferent; the number

pretenses of public good, first enrage their countrymen into a frenzy of passion, and then advance their own influence and interest, by gratifying the passion, which they themselves have basely excited.

Hitherto *Great Britain* has been contented with her prosperity. Moderation has been the rule of her conduct. But now, a general humane people, that so often has protected the liberty of strangers,

---

of *English* merchants very small, and the whole shipping of the nation much inferior to what now belongs to the Northern Colonies only. *These are certain facts.* But since their establishment, our condition has altered for the better, almost to a degree beyond credibility—Our MANUFACTURES are prodigiously increased, chiefly by the demand for them in the plantations, where they AT LEAST TAKE OFF ONE HALF, and supply us with many valuable commodities for exportation, which is as great an emolument to the mother kingdom, as to the plantations themselves." (POSTLETHWAYT's *Univ. Dict. of Trade and Commerce*)

"Most of the nations of *Europe* have interfered with us, more or less, in divers of our staple manufactures, within half a century, not only in our woolen, but in our lead and tin manufactures, as well as our fisheries." (POSTLETHWAYT, *ibid.*)

"The inhabitants of our colonies, by carrying on a trade with their *foreign neighbors,* do not only occasion a *greater quantity of the goods and merchandises* of Europe *being sent from hence to them,* and a greater quantity of the product of America to be sent from them hither, *which would otherwise be carried from, and brought* to Europe *by foreigners,* but an increase of the seamen and navigation in those parts, which is of great strength and security, as well as of great advantage to our plantations in general. And though *some of our colonies* are not only for preventing the *importations of all goods of the same species they produce,* but suffer particular planters to *keep great runs of land in their possession uncultivated,* with design to prevent new settlements, whereby they imagine the prices of their commodities may be affected; yet if it be considered, that the markets of *Great Britain* depend on the markets of ALL *Europe in general,* and that the *European* markets in *general* depend on the proportion between the *annual consumption* and the *whole quantity* of each species *annually produced* by ALL *nations;* it must follow, that whether we or foreigners are the producers, carriers, importers and exporters of *American* produce, yet their respective prices in *each colony* (the difference of freight, customs and importations considered) will always bear proportion to the *general consumption* of the *whole quantity* of each sort, *produced in all colonies,* and *in all parts,* allowing only for the usual contingencies that trade and commerce, agriculture and manufacturers, are liable to in all countries." (POSTLETHWAYT, *ibid.*)

"It is certain, that from the very time *Sir Walter Raleigh,* the father of our *English* colonies, and his associates, first projected these establishments, there have been persons who have found an interest, in *misrepresenting,* or lessening the value of them—The attempts were called *chimerical* and dangerous. Afterwards many malignant suggestions were made about sacrificing so many *Englishmen* to the obstinate desire of settling colonies in countries which then produced very little advantage. But as these difficulties were gradually surmounted, those complaints vanished. No sooner were *these lamentations* over, but *others* arose in their stead; when it could be no longer said, that the colonies were *useless,* it was alleged that they were not *useful enough* to their mother country; that

is inflamed into an attempt to tear a privilege from her own children, which, if executed, must, in their opinion, sink them into slaves: AND FOR WHAT? For a pernicious power, not necessary to her, as her own experience may convince her; but horribly dreadful and detestable to them.

It seems extremely probable, that when cool, dispassionate pos-

---

while we were loaded with taxes, they were absolutely free; that the *planters* lived like *princes,* while the inhabitants of *England* labored hard for a tolerable subsistence." (POSTLETHWAYT, *ibid.*)

"Before the settlement of these colonies," says *Postlethwayt,* "our manufactures were few, and those but indifferent. In those days we had not only our naval stores, but our ships from our neighbors. *Germany* furnished us with all things of metal, even to nails. Wine, paper, linens, and a thousand other things, came from *France. Portugal* supplied us with sugar; all the products of *America* were poured into us from *Spain;* and the *Venetians* and *Genoese* retailed to us the commodities of the *East Indies,* at their own price."

"If it be asked whether foreigners, for what goods they take of us, do not pay on *that consumption* a great portion of our taxes? It is admitted they do." (POSTLETHWAYT'S *Great Britain's True System*)

"If we are afraid that one day or other the colonies will revolt, and set up for themselves, as some seem to apprehend, let us not *drive* them to a *necessity* to *feel* themselves independent of us; as they *will* do, the moment they perceive that THEY CAN BE SUPPLIED WITH ALL THINGS FROM WITHIN THEMSELVES, and do not need our assistance. If we would keep them still dependent upon their mother country, and, in some respects, *subservient* to her *views* and welfare; let us make it their INTEREST always to be so." (TUCKER *on Trade*)

"Our colonies, while they have *English* blood in their veins, and have relations in *England,* and WHILE THEY CAN GET BY TRADING WITH US, the *stronger* and *greater* they grow, the *more* this *crown* and *kingdom* will *get* by them; and nothing but such an arbitrary power as shall make them desperate, can bring them to rebel." (DAVENANT *on the Plantation Trade*)

"The Northern colonies are not upon the same footing as those of the South; and having a worse soil to improve, they must find the recompense some other way, which only can be in property and dominion: Upon which score, any INNOVATIONS in the form of government there, should be cautiously examined, for fear of entering upon measures, by which the industry of the inhabitants be quite discouraged. 'Tis ALWAYS UNFORTUNATE for a people, either by CONSENT, or upon COMPULSION, to depart from their PRIMITIVE INSTITUTIONS, and THOSE FUNDAMENTALS, by which they were FIRST UNITED TOGETHER." (*Idem*) The most effectual way of *uniting* the colonies, is to make it their common interest to oppose the designs and attempts of *Great Britain.*

"All wise states will well consider how to preserve the advantages arising from colonies, and avoid the evils. And I conceive that there can be but TWO ways in nature to hinder them from throwing off their dependence; *one,* to keep it out of their *power,* and the *other,* out of their *will.* The *first* must be by *force;* and the *latter,* by *using them well,* and keeping them employed in such productions, and making such manufactures, as will

terity, shall consider the affectionate intercourse, the reciprocal benefits, and the unsuspecting confidence, that have subsisted between these colonies and their parent country, for such a length of time, they will execrate, with the bitterest curses, the infamous memory of those men, whose pestilential ambition unnecessarily, wantonly, cruelly, first opened the forces of civil discord between them; first turned their love into jealousy; and first taught these provinces, filled with grief and anxiety, to inquire—

Mens ubi materna est?

Where is maternal affection?

A Farmer

---

support themselves and their families comfortably, *and procure them wealth too,* and at least not prejudice their mother country.

"*Force* can never be used effectually to answer the end, *without destroying the colonies themselves.* Liberty and encouragement are necessary to carry people thither, and to keep them together when they are there; and violence will hinder both. Any body of troops, considerable enough to awe them, and keep them in subjection, under the direction too of a needy governor, often sent thither to make his fortune, and at such a distance from any application for redress, will soon put an end to all planting, and leave the country to the soldiers alone, and if it did not, *would eat up all the profit of the colony.* For this reason, arbitrary countries have not been equally successful in planting colonies with free ones; and what they have done in that kind, has either been by force, at a vast expense, or *by departing from the nature of their government,* and *giving such privileges to planters as were denied to their other subjects.* And I dare say, that a few prudent laws, and a little prudent conduct, would soon give us far the greatest share of the riches of all *America,* perhaps drive many of the other nations out of it, or into our colonies for shelter.

"There are *so many exigencies* in all states, *so many foreign wars,* and *domestic disturbances,* that these colonies CAN NEVER WANT OPPORTUNITIES, if they watch for them, *to do what they shall find their interest to do;* and therefore we ought to take all the precautions in our power, that it shall never be *their interest* to act against that of their native country; an evil which can no other-wise be averted, than by keeping them *fully employed* in such trades *as will increase their own* as well as our wealth; for it is much to be feared, if we do not find employment for them, they may find it for us; the interest of the mother country, is always to keep them dependent, and so employed; and it requires all her addresses to do it; and it is certainly more *easily* and *effectually* done by *gentle* and *insensible* methods, than by *power* alone." (CATO's *Letters*)

LETTER VI

My dear Countrymen,

It may perhaps be objected against the arguments that have been offered to the public, concerning the legal power of the parliament, "that it has always exercised the power of improving duties, for the purposes of raising a revenue on the productions of these colonies carried to Great Britain, which may be called a tax on them." To this objection I answer, that this is no violation of the rights of the colonies, it being implied in the relation between them and *Great Britain,* that they should not carry such commodities to other nations, as should enable them to interfere with the mother country. The imposition of duties on these commodities, when brought to her, is only a consequence of her parental right; and if the point is thoroughly examined, the duties will be found to be laid on the people of the mother country. Whatever they are, they must proportionably raise the price of the goods, and consequently must be paid by the consumers. In this light they were considered by the parliament in the 25th Charles II. Chap. 7, Sect. 2, which says, that the productions of the plantations were carried from one to another free from all customs, "while the subjects of this your kingdom of *England* have paid *great customs and impositions for what of them have been* SPENT HERE," etc.

Besides, if *Great Britain* exports these commodities again, the duties will injure her own trade, so that she cannot hurt us, without plainly and immediately hurting herself; and this is our check against her acting arbitrarily in this respect.

It may be perhaps further objected,* "that it being granted that

* If any one should observe that no opposition has been made to the legality of the 4th Geo. III. Chap. 15, which is the FIRST act of parliament that ever imposed duties on the importations in *America,* for the *expressed* purpose of raising a revenue there; I answer—First, That tho' the act expressly mentions the raising of a revenue in *America,* yet it seems that it had as much in view the "improving and securing the trade between the same and *Great Britain,*" which words are part of its title; And the preamble says,

statutes made for regulating trade, are binding upon us, it will be difficult for any persons, but the makers of the laws, to determine, which of them are made for the regulating of trade, and which for raising a revenue; and that from hence may arise confusion."

To this I answer, that the objection is of no force in the present case, or such as resemble it; because the act now in question, is formed expressly FOR THE SOLE PURPOSE OF RAISING A REVENUE.

However, supposing the design of parliament had not been expressed, the objection seems to me of no weight, with regard to the influence which those who may make it, might expect it ought to have on the conduct of these colonies.

It is true that *impositions for raising a revenue*, may be hereafter called *regulations of trade:* But names will not change the nature of things. Indeed we ought firmly to believe, what is an undoubted truth, confirmed by the unhappy experience of many states heretofore free, that UNLESS THE MOST WATCHFUL ATTENTION BE EXERTED, A NEW SERVITUDE MAY BE SLIPPED UPON US, UNDER THE SANCTION OF USUAL AND RESPECTABLE TERMS.

Thus the Caesars ruined the Roman liberty, under the titles of

---

"Whereas it is expedient that new provisions and regulations should be established for improving the revenue of this kingdom, and *for extending and securing the navigation and commerce between* Great Britain and *your Majesty's dominions* in America, which by the peace have been so happily extended and enlarged," etc. Secondly, All the duties mentioned in that act are imposed solely on the *productions and manufactures of foreign countries*, and not a single duty laid on any production or manufacture of our mother country. Thirdly, The authority of the provincial assemblies is not therein so plainly *attached* as by the last act, which makes provision for defraying the charges of the "administration of justice," and the intention of the 4th Geo. III. Chap. 15, was not as much *to regulate trade*, as *to raise a revenue*, the minds of the people here were wholly engrossed by the terror of the *Stamp Act*, then impending over them, about the intention of which there could be *no doubt*.

These reasons so far distinguish the 4th Geo. III. Chap. 15, from the last act, that it is not to be wondered at, that the first should have been submitted to, tho' the last should excite the more universal and spirited opposition. For *this* will be found, on the strictest examination, to be, in the *principle* on which it is founded, and in the *consequences* that must attend it, if possible, more destructive than the *Stamp Act*. It is, to speak plainly, a *prodigy* in our laws; not having one *British* feature.

tribunicial and *dictatorial* authorities—old and venerable dignities, known in the most flourishing times of freedom. In imitation of the same policy, James II when he *meant* to establish popery, *talked* of liberty of conscience, the most sacred of all liberties; and had thereby almost deceived the Dissenters into destruction.

All artful rulers, who strive to extend their power beyond its just limits, endeavor to give to their attempts as much semblance of legality as possible. Those who succeed them may venture to go a little further; for each new encroachment will be strengthened by a former. "That which is now supported by examples, growing old, will become an example itself,"* and thus support fresh usurpations.

A FREE people therefore can never be too quick in observing, nor too firm in opposing the beginnings of *alteration* either in *form* or *reality*, respecting institutions formed for their security. The first kind of alteration leads to the last: Yet, on the other hand, nothing is more certain, than that the *forms* of liberty may be retained, when the *substance* is gone. In government, as well as in religion, "The *letter* killeth, but the *spirit* giveth life."†

I will beg leave to enforce this remark by a few instances. The crown, by the constitution, has the prerogative of creating peers. The existence of that order, in due number and dignity, is essential to the constitution; and if the crown did not exercise that prerogative, the peerage must have long since decreased so much as to have lost its proper influence. Suppose a prince, for some unjust purposes, should, from time to time, advance so many needy, profligate wretches to that rank, that all the independence of the house of lords should be destroyed; there would then be a manifest violation of the constitution, *under the appearance of using legal prerogative.*

The house of commons claims the privilege of forming all money bills, and will not suffer either of the other branches of the legislature to add to, or alter them; contending that their power simply extends to an acceptance or rejection of them. This privilege appears to be just: But under pretense of this just privilege, the house of commons

* Tacitus.

† II Corinthians 3:6.

has claimed a licence of tacking to money bills, clauses relating to things of a totally different kind, and thus forcing them in a manner on the king and lords. This seems to be an abuse of that privilege, and it may be vastly more abused. Suppose a future house influenced by some displaced, discontented demagogues—in a time of danger, should tack to a money bill, something so injurious to the king and peers, that they would not assent to it, and yet the commons should obstinately insist on it; the whole kingdom would be exposed to ruin by them, *under the appearance of maintaining a valuable privilege.*

In these cases it might be difficult for a while to determine, whether the king intended to exercise his prerogative in a constitutional manner or not; or whether the commons insisted on their demand factiously, or for the public good: But surely the conduct of the crown, or of the house, would in time sufficiently explain itself.

Ought not the people therefore to watch? to observe facts? to search into causes? to investigate designs? And have they not a right of *JUDGING* from the evidence before them, on no slighter points than their *liberty* and *happiness?* It would be less than trifling, whenever a *British* government is established, to make use of any arguments to prove such a right. It is sufficient to remind the reader of the day, on the anniversary of which the first of these letters is dated.

I will now apply what has been said to the present question.

The *nature* of any impositions laid by parliament on these colonies, must determine the *design* in laying them. It may not be easy in every instance to discover that design. Whenever it is doubtful, I think submission cannot be dangerous; nay, it must be right, for, in my opinion, there is no privilege these colonies claim, which they ought in *duty* and *prudence* more earnestly to maintain and defend, than the authority of the *British* parliament to regulate the trade of all her dominions. Without this authority, the benefits she enjoys from our commerce, must be lost to her: The blessings we enjoy from our dependence upon her, must be lost to us. Her strength must decay; her glory vanish; and she cannot suffer without our partaking in her misfortune. *Let us therefore cherish her interests as our own, and give her everything, that it becomes* FREEMEN *to give or to receive.*

The *nature* of any impositions she may lay upon us may, in

general, be known, by considering how far they relate to the preserving, in due order, at the connection between the several parts of the *British* empire. One thing we may be assured of, which is this—Whenever she imposes duties on commodities, to be paid only upon their exportation from *Great Britain* to these colonies, it is not a regulation of trade, but a design to raise a revenue upon us. Other instances may happen, which it may not be necessary at present to dwell on. I hope these colonies will never, to their latest existence, want understanding sufficient to discover the intentions of those who rule over them, nor the resolution necessary for asserting their interests. They will always have the same rights, that all free states have, of judging when their privileges are invaded, and of using all prudent measures for preserving them.

Quocirca vivite fortes
Fortiaque adversis opponite pectora rebus.

Wherefore keep up your spirits, and gallantly
oppose this adverse course of affairs.

A Farmer

LETTER VII

My dear Countrymen,

This letter is intended more particularly for such of you, whose employments in life may have prevented your attending to the consideration of some points that are of great and public importance: For many such persons there must be even in these colonies, where the inhabitants in general are more intelligent than any other people whatever, as has been remarked by strangers, and it seems with reason.

Some of you, perhaps, filled, as I know your breasts are, with loyalty to our most excellent Prince, and with love to our dear mother country, may feel yourselves inclined, by the affections of your hearts, to approve every action of those whom you so much venerate and esteem. A prejudice thus flowing from goodness of disposition, is amiable indeed. I wish it could be indulged without danger. Did I think this possible, the error should have been adopted, and not opposed by me. But in truth, all men are subject to the frailties of nature; and therefore whatever regard we entertain for the persons of those who govern us, we should always remember that their conduct, as *rulers,* may be influenced by human infirmities.

When any laws, injurious to these colonies, are passed, we cannot suppose, that any injury was intended us by his Majesty, or the Lords. For the assent of the crown and peers to laws, seems, as far as I am able to judge, to have been vested in them, more for their own security, than for any other purpose. On the other hand, it is the particular business of the people, to inquire and discover what regulations are useful for themselves, and to digest and present them in the form of bills, to the other orders, to have them enacted into laws. Where these laws are to bind *themselves,* it may be expected, that the house of commons will very carefully consider them: But when they are making laws that are not designed to bind *themselves,* we cannot imagine that their deliberations will be as cautious* and scrupulous, as in their own case.

* Many remarkable instances might be produced of the extraordinary inattention with which bills of great importance, concerning these colonies, have passed in parliament; which is owing, as it is supposed, to the bills being brought in by the persons who have points to carry, so artfully framed, that it is not easy for the members in general, in the haste of business, to discover their tendency.

The following instances show the truth of this remark. When Mr. *Greenville,* in the violence of reformation, formed the 4th Geo. III. Chap. 15th, for regulating the *American* trade, the word "*Ireland*" was dropped in the clause relating to our iron and lumber, so that we could send these articles to no part of *Europe,* but to Great Britain. This was so unreasonable a restriction, and so contrary to the sentiments of the legislature for many years before, that it is surprising it should not have been taken notice of in the house. However the bill passed into a law. But when the matter was explained, this restriction was taken off by a subsequent act. I cannot positively say how long after the taking off of this restriction, as I have not the act, but I think, in less than 18 months, another act of parliament passed, in which the word "*Ireland*" was left out, just as it had been before. The matter being a second time explained, was a second time regulated.

I am told, that there is a wonderful address frequently used in carrying points in the house of commons, by persons experienced in these affairs—That opportunities are watched—and sometimes votes are passed, that if all the members had been present, would have been rejected by a great majority. Certain it is, that when a powerful and artful man has determined on any measure against these colonies, he has always succeeded in his attempt. Perhaps therefore it will be proper for us, whenever any oppressive act affecting us is passed, to attribute it to the inattention of the members of the house of commons, and to the malevolence or ambition of some factious great man, rather than to any other cause.

Now I do verily believe, that the late act of parliament, imposing duties on paper, etc. was formed by Mr. *Greenville,* and his party, because it is evidently a part of that plan, by which he endeavored to render himself POPULAR at home; and I do also believe, that not one half of the members of the house of commons, even of those who heard it read, did perceive how destructive it was to *American* freedom. For this reason, as it is usual in *Great Britain,* to consider the King's speech as the speech of the ministry, it may be right here to consider this act as the act of a *party*—perhaps I should speak more properly, if I was to use another term.

Now if it be considered, that the omission mentioned struck off with ONE word so VERY GREAT A PART OF OUR TRADE, it must appear *remarkable;* and equally so is the method, by which *Rice* became an enumerated commodity.

"The enumeration was obtained (says Mr. *Gee*) by one *Cole,* a Captain of a ship, employed by a company then trading to *Carolina;* for several ships going from *England* thither, and purchasing rice for *Portugal,* prevented the *aforesaid Captain* of a loading. Upon his coming home, he possessed one Mr. *Lowndes,* a member of parliament (*who was very frequently employed to prepare bills*) with an opinion, that carrying rice directly to *Portugal,* was a prejudice to the trade of *England,* and PRIVATELY got a clause into an act, to make it an enumerated commodity; *by which means he secured a freight to himself.* BUT THE CONSEQUENCE PROVED A VAST LOSS TO THE NATION." I find that this clause, "PRIVATELY got into an act," FOR THE BENEFIT OF CAPTAIN COLE, to the "VAST LOSS OF THE NATION," is foisted into the 3d and 4th *Anne,* Chap. 5th, intitled, "An act for granting to her Majesty a further subsidy on wines and merchandises imported," with which it has no more connection, than with 34th *Edward* I. the 34th and 35th of *Henry* VIII, and the 25th of *Charles* II. WHICH PROVIDE, THAT NO PERSON SHALL BE TAXED BUT BY HIMSELF OR HIS REPRESENTATIVE.

There are two ways of laying taxes. One is, by imposing a certain sum on particular kinds of property, to be paid by the *user* or *consumer*, or by rating the *person* at a certain sum. The other is, by imposing a certain sum on particular kinds of property, to be paid by the seller.

When a man pays the first sort of tax, he *knows with certainty*, that he pays so much money for a tax. The *consideration* for which he pays it, is remote, and, it may be, does not occur to him. He is sensible too, that he is *commanded and obliged* to pay it *as a tax;* and therefore people are apt to be displeased with this sort of tax.

The other sort of tax is submitted to in a very different manner. The purchaser of any article, very seldom reflects that the seller raises his price, so as to indemnify himself for the tax *he* has paid. He knows that the prices of things are continually fluctuating, and if he thinks about the tax, he thinks at the same time, in all probability, that he *might* have paid as much, if the article he buys had not been taxed. He gets something *visible* and *agreeable* for his money; and tax and price are so confounded together, that he cannot separate, or does not choose to take the trouble of separating them.

This mode of taxation therefore is the mode suited to arbitrary and oppressive governments. The love of liberty is so natural to the human heart, that unfeeling tyrants think themselves obliged to accommodate their schemes as much as they can to the appearance of justice and reason, and to deceive those whom they resolve to destroy, or oppress, by presenting to them a miserable picture of freedom, when the inestimable original is lost.

This policy did not escape the cruel and rapacious NERO. That monster, apprehensive that his crimes might endanger his authority and life, thought proper to do some popular acts, to secure the obedience of his subjects. Among other things, says *Tacitus,* "he remitted the twenty-fifth part of the price on the sale of slaves, but rather in *show* than *reality;* for the seller being ordered to pay it, it became part of the price to the buyer."*

This is the reflection of the judicious *Historian;* but the deluded *people* gave their infamous Emperor full credit for his false generosity.

* *Tacitus's Ann.* Book 13, § 13.

Other nations have been treated in the same manner the *Romans* were. The honest, industrious *Germans,* who are settled in different parts of this continent, can inform us, that it was this sort of tax that drove them from their native land to our woods, at that time the seats of perfect and undisturbed freedom.

Their Princes, inflamed by the lust of power, and the lust of avarice, two furies that the more they are gorged, the more hungry they grow, transgressed the bounds they ought, in regard to themselves, to have observed. To keep up the deception in the minds of subjects, "there must be," says a very learned author,* "some proportion between the impost and the value of the commodity; wherefore there ought not to be an excessive duty upon merchandise of little value. There are countries in which the duty exceeds seventeen or eighteen times the value of the commodity. In this case the Prince removes the illusion. His subjects plainly see they are dealt with in an unreasonable manner, which renders them most exquisitely sensible of their slavish situation." From hence it appears, that subjects may be ground down into misery by this sort of taxation, as well as by the former. They will be as much impoverished, if their money is taken from them in this way as in the other; and that it will be taken, may be more evident, by attending to a few more considerations.

The merchant or importer, who pays the duty at first, will not consent to be so much money out of pocket. He therefore proportionally raises the price of his goods. It may then be said to be a contest between him and the person offering to buy, who shall lose the duty. This must be decided by the nature of the commodities, and the purchaser's demand for them. If they are mere luxuries, he is at liberty to do as he pleases, and if he buys, he does it voluntarily: But if they are absolute *necessaries,* or *conveniences,* which use and custom have made requisite for the comfort of life, and which he is not permitted, by the power imposing the duty, to get *elsewhere,* there the seller has a plain advantage, and the buyer *must* pay the duty. In fact, the seller is nothing less than a collector of the tax for the power that imposed it. If these duties then are extended to the necessaries and conveniences

* *Montesquieu's Spirit of Laws, Book* 13, Chap. 8.

of life in general, and enormously increased, the people must at length become indeed "most exquisitely sensible of their slavish situation." Their happiness therefore entirely depends on the moderation of those who have authority to impose the duties.

I shall now apply these observations to the late act of parliament. Certain duties are thereby imposed on paper and glass, imported into these colonies. By the laws of *Great Britain* we are prohibited to get these articles from any other part of the world. We cannot at present, nor for many years to come, tho' we should apply ourselves to these manufacturers with the utmost industry, make enough ourselves for our own use. That paper and glass are not only convenient, but absolutely necessary for us, I imagine very few will contend. Some perhaps, who think mankind grew wicked and luxurious, as soon as they found out another way of communicating their sentiments than by speech, and another way of dwelling than in caves, may advance so whimsical an opinion. But I presume no body will take the unnecessary trouble of refuting them.

From these remarks I think it evident, that we *must* use paper and glass; that what we use, *must* be *British;* and that we must pay the duties imposed, unless those who sell these articles, are so generous as to make us presents of the duties they pay.

Some persons may think this act of no consequence, because the duties are so *small.* A fatal error. *That* is the very circumstance most alarming to me. For I am convinced, that the authors of this law would never have obtained an act to raise so trifling a sum as it must do, had they not intended by *it* to establish a *precedent* for future use. To console ourselves with the smallness of the duties, is to walk deliberately into the snare that is set for us, praising the *neatness* of the workmanship. Suppose the duties imposed by the late act could be paid by these distressed colonies with the utmost ease, and that the purposes to which they are to be applied, were the most reasonable and equitable that can be conceived, the contrary of which I hope to demonstrate before these letters are concluded; yet even in such a supposed case, these colonies ought to regard the act with abhorrence. For WHO ARE A FREE PEOPLE? Not *those,* over whom government is reasonable and equitably exercised, but *those,* who live under a government so *constitutionally checked and controlled,* that proper provision is made against its being otherwise exercised.

The late act is founded on the destruction of this constitutional security. If the parliament have a right to lay a duty of Four Shillings and Eight-pence on a hundred weight of glass, or a ream of paper, they have a right to lay a duty of any other sum on either. They may raise the duty, as the author before quoted says has been done in some countries, till it "exceeds seventeen or eighteen times the value of the commodity." In short, if they have a right *to* levy a tax of *one penny* upon us, they have a right to levy a *million* upon us: For where does their right stop? At any given number of Pence, Shillings or Pounds? To attempt to limit their right, after granting it to exist at all, is as contrary to reason—as granting it to exist at all, is contrary to justice. If *they* have any right to tax *us*—then, whether *our own money* shall continue in *our own pockets* or not, depends no longer on *us,* but on *them.* "There is nothing which" we "can call our own; or, to use the words of Mr. Locke—WHAT PROPERTY HAVE" WE "IN THAT, WHICH ANOTHER MAY, BY RIGHT, TAKE, WHEN HE PLEASES, TO HIMSELF?"*

These duties, which will inevitably be levied upon us—which are now levying upon us—are *expressly* laid FOR THE SOLE PURPOSE OF TAKING MONEY. This is the true definition of "*taxes.*" They are therefore *taxes.* This money is to be taken from *us. We* are therefore taxed. *Those* who are *taxed* without their own consent, expressed by themselves or their representatives, are *slaves. We are taxed* without our own consent, expressed by ourselves or our representatives. *We* are therefore—SLAVES.†

* Lord *Cambden's* speech.

† "It is my opinion, that this kingdom has no right to lay A TAX upon the colonies"—"The *Americans* are the SONS, not the BASTARDS of *England*"—"The distinction between LEGISLATION and TAXATION is essentially necessary to liberty"—"The COMMONS of *America,* represented in their several assemblies, have ever been in possession of this their constitutional right, of GIVING AND GRANTING THEIR OWN MONEY. They would have been SLAVES, if they had not enjoyed it." "The idea of a *virtual representation* of *America* in this house, is the most contemptible idea that ever entered into the head of man—It does not deserve a serious refutation." (Mr. Pitt's *Speech on the Stamp-Act*)

Miserabile vulgus.

A miserable tribe.

A Farmer

That great and excellent man Lord *Cambden,* maintains the same opinion. His speech in the house of peers, on the declaratory bill of the sovereignty of *Great Britain* over the colonies, has lately appeared in our papers. The following extracts so perfectly agree with, and confirm the sentiments avowed in these letters, that it is hoped the inserting them in this note will be excused.

"As the affair is of the *utmost importance,* and in its consequences may involve the *fate of kingdoms,* I took the strictest review of my arguments; I re-examined all my authorities; fully determined, if I found myself mistaken, publicly to own my mistake, and give up my opinion: But my searches have more and more convinced me, that the *British* parliament have NO RIGHT TO TAX the *Americans*"—"Nor is the doctrine new; it is as old as the constitution; it grew up with it; indeed it is its support"—"TAXATION and REPRESENTATION are inseparably united. GOD hath joined them: No *British* parliament can separate them: To endeavor to do it, is to stab our vitals."

"My position is this—I repeat it—I will maintain it to my last hour—TAXATION and REPRESENTATION are inseparable—this position is founded on the laws of nature; it is more, it is itself AN ETERNAL LAW OF NATURE; for whatever is a man's own, is absolutely his own; NO MAN HATH A RIGHT TO TAKE IT FROM HIM WITHOUT HIS CONSENT, either expressed by himself or representative; *whoever attempts to do it, attempts an injury;* WHOEVER DOES IT, COMMITS A ROBBERY; HE THROWS DOWN THE DISTINCTION BETWEEN LIBERTY AND SLAVERY." "There is not a *blade of grass,* which, when taxed, *was not taxed by the consent of the proprietor.*" "The forefathers of the *Americans* did not leave their native country, and subject themselves to every danger and distress, TO BE REDUCED TO A STATE OF SLAVERY. They did not give up their rights: They looked for protection, and *not for* CHAINS, from their mother country. By her they expected to be defended in the possession of their property, and not to be deprived of it: For should the present power continue, THERE IS NOTHING WHICH THEY CAN CALL THEIR OWN; or, to use the words of Mr. Locke, "WHAT PROPERTY HAVE THEY IN THAT, WHICH ANOTHER MAY, BY RIGHT, TAKE, WHEN HE PLEASES, TO HIMSELF?"

It is impossible to read this speech, and Mr. *Pitt's,* and not be charmed with the generous zeal for the rights of mankind that glows in every sentence. These great and good men, animated by the subject they speak upon, seem to rise above all the former glorious exertions of their abilities. A foreigner might be tempted to think they are *Americans,* asserting, with all the ardor of patriotism, and all the anxiety of apprehension, the cause of their native land—and not *Britons,* striving to stop their mistaken countrymen from oppressing others. Their reasoning is not only just—it is, as Mr. *Hume* says of the eloquence of Demosthenes, "vehement." It is disdain, anger, boldness, freedom, involved in a continual stream of argument.

LETTER VIII

My dear Countrymen,

In my opinion, a dangerous example is set in the last act relating to these colonies. The power of parliament to levy money upon us for raising a revenue, is therein *avowed* and *exerted.* Regarding the act on this single principle, I must again repeat, and I think it my duty to repeat, that to me it appears to be *unconstitutional.*

No man, who considers the conduct of the parliament since the repeal of the *Stamp Act,* and the disposition of many people at home, can doubt, that the chief object of attention there, is, to use Mr. *Greenville's* expression, "providing that the DEPENDENCE and OBEDIENCE of the colonies be asserted and maintained."

Under the influence of this notion, instantly on repealing the *Stamp Act,* an act passed, declaring the power of parliament to bind these colonies *in all cases whatever.* This however was only planting a barren tree, that cast a *shade* indeed over the colonies, but yielded no *fruit.* It being determined to enforce the authority on which the *Stamp Act* was founded, the parliament having never renounced the right, as Mr. *Pitt* advised them to do; and it being thought proper to disguise that authority in such a manner, as not again to alarm the colonies; some little time was required to find a method, by which both these points should be united. At last the ingenuity of Mr. *Greenville* and his party accomplished the matter, as it was thought, in "an act for granting certain duties in the British colonies and plantations in America, for allowing drawbacks," etc. which is the title of the act laying duties on paper, etc.

The parliament having several times before imposed duties to be paid in *America,* IT WAS EXPECTED, NO DOUBT, THAT THE REPETITION OF SUCH A MEASURE WOULD BE PASSED OVER, AS A USUAL THING. But to have done this, without expressly "asserting and maintaining" the power of parliament to take our money without our consent, and to apply it as they please, would not have been, in Mr. *Greenville's* opinion, sufficiently declarative of its supremacy, nor sufficiently depressive of *American* freedom.

THEREFORE it is, that in this memorable act we find it expressly "provided," that money shall be levied upon us without our consent, for PURPOSES, that render it, *if possible*, more dreadful than the *Stamp Act.*

That act, alarming as it was, declared, the money thereby to be raised, should be applied "towards defraying the expenses of defending, protecting and securing the *British* colonies and plantations in *America*": And it is evident from the whole act, that by the word "*British,*" were intended colonies and plantations *settled by* British *people,* and not generally, *those subject to the* British *crown.* That act therefore seemed to have something gentle and kind in its intention, and to aim only at *our own welfare:* But the act now objected to, imposes duties upon the *British* colonies, "to defray the expenses of defending, protecting and securing *his Majesty's* DOMINIONS *in* America."

What a *change* of words! What an *incomputable addition* to the expenses intended by the *STAMP ACT! "His Majesty's* DOMINIONS" comprehend not only *the* British *colonies,* but also *the conquered provinces of* Canada *and* Florida, *and the* British *garrisons* of Nova-Scotia; for *these* do not deserve the name of *colonies.*

What justice is there in making us pay for "defending, protecting and securing" THESE PLACES? What benefit *can* WE, or *have* WE ever derived *from them?* None of them was conquered *for* US; nor will "be defended, protected or secured" *for* US.

In fact, however advantageous the subduing or keeping any of these countries may be to *Great Britain,* the acquisition is greatly injurious to these colonies. Our chief property consists in *lands.* These would have been of much greater value, if such prodigious additions had not been made to the *British* territories on this continent. The natural increase of our own people, if confined within the colonies, would have raised the value still higher and higher every fifteen or twenty years: Besides, we should have lived more compactly together, and have been therefore more able to resist any enemy. But now the inhabitants will be thinly scattered over an immense region, as those who want settlements, will choose to make new ones, rather than pay great prices for old ones.

These are the consequences to the colonies, of the hearty assistance they gave to *Great Britain* in the late war—a war *undertaken solely for her own benefit.* The objects of it were, the securing to herself of the rich tracts of land on the back of these colonies, with the *Indian* trade; and *Nova-Scotia,* with the fishery. *These, and much more, has that kingdom gained;* but the *inferior animals,* that hunted with the lion, have been amply rewarded for all the sweat and blood their loyalty cost them, by the honor of having sweated and bled in such company.

I will not go so far as to say, that *Canada* and *Nova-Scotia* are curbs on *New England;* the *chain of forts* through the back-woods, of the *Middle Provinces;* and *Florida,* on the rest: But I will venture to say, that if the products of *Canada, Nova-Scotia,* and *Florida,* deserve any consideration, the two first of them are only rivals of our Northern Colonies, and the other of our Southern.

It has been said, that without the conquest of these countries, the colonies could not have been "protected, defended and secured." If that is true, it may with as much propriety be said, that *Great Britain* could not have been "defended, protected and secured," without that conquest: For the colonies are parts of her empire, which it *as much* concerns *her* as *them* to keep out of the hands of any other power.

But these colonies, when they were much weaker, defended themselves, before this Conquest was made; and could again do it, against any that might properly be called *their* Enemies. If *France* and *Spain* indeed should attack them, *as members of the* British *empire,* perhaps they might be distressed; but it would be in a *British* quarrel.

The largest account I have seen of the number of people in *Canada,* does not make them exceed *90,000. Florida* can hardly be said to have any inhabitants. It is computed that there are in our colonies *3,000,000. Our* force therefore must increase with a disproportion to the growth of *their* strength, that would render us very safe.

This being the state of the case, I cannot think it just that these colonies, laboring under so many misfortunes, should be loaded with *taxes,* to maintain countries, not only not useful, but hurtful to them. The support of *Canada* and *Florida* cost yearly, it is said, half a million sterling. From hence, we may make some guess of the load that is to be laid *upon* US; for WE are not only to "defend, protect and secure" *them,* but also to make "an adequate provision for defraying the charge of the administration of justice, and the support of civil government, in such provinces where it shall be found necessary."

Not one of the provinces of *Canada, Nova-Scotia,* or *Florida,* has ever defrayed *these expenses within itself:* And if the duties imposed by the last statute are collected, *all of them together,* according to the best information I can get, will not pay *one quarter as much as* Pennsylvania *alone.* So that the *British colonies* are to be drained of the rewards of their labor, to cherish the scorching sands of *Florida,* and the icy rocks of *Canada* and *Nova-Scotia,* which never will return to us one farthing that we send to them.

GREAT BRITAIN—I mean, the ministry in *Great Britain,* has cantoned *Canada* and *Florida* out into *five* or *six* governments, and may form *as many more.* There now are *fourteen* or *fifteen* regiments on this continent; and there soon may be *as many more.* To make "an adequate provision" FOR ALL THESE EXPENSES, is, no doubt, to be the *inheritance* of the colonies.

Can any man believe that the duties upon paper, etc. are the *last* that will be laid for these purposes? It is in vain to hope, that because it is imprudent to lay duties on the exportation of manufactures from a mother country to colonies, as it may promote manufactures among them, that this consideration will prevent such a measure.

Ambitious, artful men have made it popular, and whatever injustice or destruction will attend it in the opinion of the colonists, at home it will be thought just and salutary.*

The people of *Great Britain* will be told, and have been told, that *they* are sinking under an immense debt—that a great part of

* "So *credulous,* as well as *obstinate,* are the people in believing *everything,* which flatters their *prevailing passion.*" (*Hume's Hist. of England*)

this debt has been contracted in defending the colonies—that these are so ungrateful and undutiful, that they will not contribute one mite to its payment—nor even to the support of the army now kept up for their "defense and security"—that they are rolling in wealth, and are of so bold and republican a spirit, that they are aiming at independence—that the only way to retain them in "obedience," is to keep a strict watch over them, and to draw off part of their riches in *taxes*—and that every burden laid upon *them,* is taking off so much from *Great Britain*—These assertions will be generally believed, and the people will be persuaded that they cannot be too angry with their colonies, as that anger will be profitable to themselves.

In truth, *Great Britain* alone receives any benefit from *Canada, Nova-Scotia and Florida;* and therefore she alone ought to maintain them. The old maxim of the law is drawn from reason and justice, and never could be more properly applied, than in this case.

Qui sentit commodum, sentire debet et onus.

They who feel the benefit, ought to feel the burden.

A Farmer

LETTER IX

My dear Countrymen,

I have made some observations on the PURPOSES for which money is to be levied upon us by the late act of parliament. I shall now offer to your consideration some further reflections on that subject: And, unless I am greatly mistaken, if these purposes are accomplished according to the *expressed* intention of the act, they will be found effectually to *supersede* that authority in our respective assemblies, which is essential to liberty. The question is not, whether some branches shall be lopped off—The axe is laid to the root of the tree; and the whole body must infallibly perish, if we remain idle spectators of the work.

No free people ever existed, or can ever exist, without keeping, to use a common, but strong expression, "the purse strings," in their own hands. Where this is the case, *they* have a *constitutional check* upon the administration, which may thereby be brought into order *without violence:* But where such a power is not lodged in the *people,* oppression proceeds uncontrolled in its career, till the governed, transported into rage, seek redress in the midst of blood and confusion.

The elegant and ingenious Mr. *Hume,* speaking of the *Anglo-Norman* government, says—"Princes and Ministers were too ignorant, to be themselves sensible of the advantage attending an equitable administration, and there was no established council or *assembly,* WHICH COULD PROTECT THE PEOPLE, and BY WITHDRAWING SUPPLIES, regularly and PEACEABLY admonish the king of his duty, and ENSURE THE EXECUTION OF THE LAWS."

Thus this great man, whose political reflections are so much admired, makes *this power* one of the foundations of liberty.

The *English* history abounds with instances, proving that *this* is the proper and successful way to obtain redress to grievances. How often have kings and ministers endeavored to throw off this legal curb upon them, by attempting to raise money by a variety of inventions, under pretense of law, without having recourse to parliament? And how often have they been brought to reason, and peaceably obliged to do justice, by the exertion of this constitutional authority of the people, vested in their representatives?

The inhabitants of these colonies have, on numberless occasions, reaped the benefit of this authority *lodged in their assemblies.*

It has been for a long time, and now is, a constant instruction to all governors, *to obtain* a PERMANENT *support for the offices of government.* But as the author of "the administration of the colonies" says, "this order of the crown is generally, if not universally, rejected by the legislatures of the colonies."

They perfectly know *how much* their grievances would be regarded, if they had *no other* method of engaging attention, than by *complaining.* Those who rule, are extremely apt to think well of the constructions made by themselves in support of their own power. *These* are frequently erroneous, and pernicious to those they govern. Dry remonstrances, to show that such constructions are wrong and oppressive, carry very little weight with them, in the opinion of persons who gratify their own inclinations in making these constructions. *They* CANNOT understand the reasoning that opposes *their* power and desires. But let it be made *their interest* to understand such reasoning—and a *wonderful light* is instantly thrown upon the matter; and then, rejected remonstrances become as clear as "proofs of holy writ."*

The three most important articles that our assemblies, or any legislatures can provide for, are, First—the defense of the society: Secondly—the administration of justice: And thirdly—the support of civil government.

Nothing can properly regulate the expense of making provision for these occasions, but the *necessities* of the society; its *abilities;* the *conveniency* of the modes of levying money in it; the *manner* in which the laws have been executed; and the *conduct* of the officers of government: *All which* are circumstances, that *cannot* possibly be properly *known,* but by the society itself; or if they should be known, *will not* probably be properly *considered* but by that society.

If money be raised upon us by *others,* without our consent, for our "defense," those who are the judges in *levying* it, must also be the judges in *applying* it. Of consequence the money *said* to be taken from us for our defense, *may be employed* to our injury. We may be chained in by a line of fortifications—obliged to pay for the building and maintaining them—and be told, that they are for our defense. With what face can we dispute the fact, after having granted that those who *apply* the money, had a right to *levy* it? For surely, it is much easier for their wisdom to understand how to apply it in the best manner, than how to levy it in the best manner. Besides, the

* Shakespeare.

right of levying is of infinitely more consequence than *that of applying.* The people of *England,* who would burst out into a fury, if the crown should attempt to *levy* money by its own authority, have always assigned to the crown the *application* of money.

As to "the administration of justice"—the judges ought, in a well regulated state, to be equally independent of the executive and legislative powers. Thus in *England,* judges hold their commissions from the crown "*during good behavior,*" and have salaries, suitable to their dignity, *settled* on them by parliament. The purity of the courts of law since this establishment, is a proof of the wisdom with which it was made.

But in these colonies, how fruitless has been every attempt to have the judges appointed "*during good behavior*"? Yet whoever considers the matter will soon perceive, that *such commissions* are beyond all comparison more necessary in these colonies, than they were in *England.*

The chief danger to the subject *there,* arose from the arbitrary *designs of the crown;* but *here,* the time may come, when we may have to contend with the *designs of the crown, and of a mighty kingdom.* What then must be our chance, when the laws of life and death are to be spoken by judges totally dependent on *that crown,* and *that kingdom*—sent over perhaps *from thence*—filled with *British prejudices*—and *backed by a* STANDING *army*—supported out of OUR OWN pockets, to "assert and maintain" OUR OWN "dependence and obedience"?

But supposing that through the extreme lenity that will prevail in the government *through all future ages,* these colonies will never behold any thing like the campaign of chief justice *Jeffereys,* yet what innumerable acts of injustice may be committed, and how fatally may the principles of liberty be sapped, by a succession of judges *utterly independent of the people?* Before such judges, the supple wretches, who cheerfully join in avowing sentiments inconsistent with freedom, will always meet with smiles; while the honest and brave men, who disdain to sacrifice their native land to their own advantage, but on every occasion boldly vindicate her cause, will constantly be regarded with frowns.

There are two other considerations relating to this head, that deserve the most serious attention.

By the late act, the officers of the customs are "impowered to enter into any HOUSE, warehouse, shop, cellar, or other place, in the *British* colonies or plantations in *America,* to search for or seize prohibited or unaccustomed goods," etc. on "writs granted by the superior or supreme court of justice, having jurisdiction within such colony or plantation respectively."

If we only reflect, that the judges of these courts are to be *during pleasure*—that they are to have "*adequate provision*" made for them, which is to continue *during their complaisant behavior*—that they may be *strangers* to these colonies—what an engine of oppression may this authority be in such hands?

I am well aware, that writs of this kind may be granted at home, under the seal of the court of exchequer: But I know also, that the greatest asserters of the rights of *Englishmen* have always strenuously contended, that *such a power* was dangerous to freedom, and expressly contrary to the common law, which ever regarded a man's *house* as his castle, or a place of perfect security.

If such power was in the least degree dangerous *there,* it must be utterly destructive to liberty *here.* For the people there have two securities against the undue exercise of this power by the crown, which are wanting with us, if the late act takes place. In the first place, if any injustice is done *there,* the person injured may bring his action against the offender, and have it tried before INDEPENDENT JUDGES, who are NO PARTIES IN COMMITTING THE INJURY. *Here* he must have it tried before DEPENDENT JUDGES, being the men WHO GRANTED THE WRIT.*

To say, that the cause is to be tried by a jury, can never reconcile men who have any idea of freedom, to *such a power.* For we know that sheriffs in almost every colony on this continent, are totally dependent on the crown; and packing of juries has been frequently

* The writs for searching houses in *England,* are to be granted "under the seal of the court of exchequer," according to the statute—and that seal is kept by the chancellor of the exchequer. 4th Inst. p. 104.

practised even in the capital of the *British* empire. Even if juries are well inclined, we have too many instances of the influence of overbearing unjust judges upon them. The brave and wise men who accomplished the revolution, thought the *independency of judges* essential to freedom.

The other security which the people have at home, but which we shall want here, is this.

If this power is abused *there,* the parliament, the grand resource of the oppressed people, is ready to afford relief. Redress of grievances must precede grants of money. But what regard can *we* expect to have paid to our assemblies, when they will not hold even the puny privilege of *French* parliaments—that of registering, before they are put in execution, the edicts that take away our money.

The second consideration above hinted at, is this. There is a confusion in our laws, that is quite unknown in *Great Britain.* As this cannot be described in a more clear or exact manner, than has been done by the ingenious author of the history of *New York,* I beg leave to use his words. "The state of our laws opens a door to much controversy. The *uncertainty,* with respect to them, RENDERS PROPERTY PRECARIOUS, and GREATLY EXPOSES US TO THE ARBITRARY DECISION OF BAD JUDGES. The common law of *England* is generally received, together with such statutes as were enacted before we had a legislature of our own; but our COURTS EXERCISE A SOVEREIGN AUTHORITY, in determining *what parts of the common and statute law* ought to be extended: For it must be admitted, that the *difference of circumstances* necessarily requires us, in some cases, *to* REJECT *the determination* of both. In many instances, they have also extended even acts of parliament, passed since we had a distinct legislature, *which is greatly adding to our confusion.* The practice of our courts is no less *uncertain than* the law. Some of the *English* rules are adopted, others rejected. Two things therefore seem to be ABSOLUTELY NECESSARY for the PUBLIC SECURITY. First, the passing an act for settling the extent of the *English* laws. Secondly, that the courts ordain a general set of rules for the regulation of the practice."

How easy it will be, under this "state of our laws," for an artful judge, to act in the most arbitrary manner, and yet cover his conduct under specious pretences; and how difficult it will be for the injured people to obtain relief, may be readily perceived. We may take a voyage of 3000 miles to complain; and after the trouble and hazard we have undergone, we may be told, that the collection of the revenue, and maintenance of the prerogative, must not be discouraged—and if the misbehavior is so gross as to admit of no justification, it may be said, that it was an error in judgment only, arising from the confusion of our laws, and the zeal of the King's servants to do their duty.

If the commissions of judges are *during the pleasure of the crown,* yet if their salaries are *during the pleasure of the people,* there will be *some check* upon their conduct. Few men will consent to draw on themselves the hatred and contempt of those among whom they live, for the empty honor of being judges. It is the sordid love of gain, that tempts men to turn their backs on virtue, and pay their homage where they ought not.

As to the third particular, "the support of civil government"—few words will be sufficient. Every man of the least understanding must know, that the executive power may be exercised in a manner so disagreeable and harassing to the people, that it is absolutely requisite, that *they* should be enabled by the gentlest method which human policy has yet been ingenious enough to invent, that is, by *shutting their hands,* to "ADMONISH" (as Mr. *Hume* says) certain persons "OF THEIR DUTY."

What shall we now think when, upon looking into the late act, we find the assemblies of these provinces thereby stripped of their authority *on these several heads?* The *declared* intention of the act is, "that a revenue should be raised IN HIS MAJESTY'S DOMINIONS IN AMERICA, for making a more certain and adequate provision *for defraying the charge of* THE ADMINISTRATION OF JUSTICE, and *the support of* CIVIL GOVERNMENT in such provinces where it shall be found necessary, and *toward further defraying the expenses of* DEFENDING, PROTECTING AND SECURING THE SAID DOMINIONS."

Let the reader pause here one moment—and reflect—whether the colony in which *he* lives, has not made such "certain and adequate provision" *for these purposes,* as is *by the colony judged suitable to its abilities, and all other circumstances.* Then let him reflect—whether if this act takes place, money is not to be raised on *that* colony *without its consent,* to make "provision" *for these purposes,* which *it does not judge to be suitable to its abilities, and all other circumstances.* Lastly, let him reflect—whether the people of that country are not in a state of the most abject slavery, *whose property may be taken from them* under the notion of right, *when they have refused to give it.*

For my part, I think I have good reason for vindicating the honor of the assemblies on this continent, by publicly asserting, that THEY *have made as "certain and adequate provision" for the purposes above mentioned, as they ought to have made,* and that it should not be presumed, that they will not do it hereafter. Why then should *these most important trusts* be wrested out of their hands? Why should they not now be permitted to enjoy that authority, which they have exercised from the first settlement of these colonies? Why should they be scandalized by this innovation, when their respective provinces are now, and will be, for several years, laboring under loads of debt, imposed on them for the very purpose now spoken of? Why should all the inhabitants of these colonies be, with the utmost indignity, treated as a herd of despicable stupid wretches, so utterly void of common sense, that they will not even make "adequate provision" for the "administration of justice, and the support of civil government" among them, or for their own "defense"—though without such "provision" every people must inevitably be overwhelmed with anarchy and destruction? Is it possible to form an idea of a slavery more *complete,* more *miserable,* more *disgraceful,* than that of a people, where *justice is administered, government exercised,* and a *standing army maintained,* AT THE EXPENSE OF THE PEOPLE, and yet WITHOUT THE LEAST DEPENDENCE UPON THEM? If we can find no relief from this infamous situation, it will be fortunate for us, if Mr. *Greenville,* setting his fertile fancy again at work, can, as by one exertion of it he has stripped us of our *property* and *liberty,* by another deprive us of so much of our *understanding;* that, unconscious of what we *have been* or *are,* and ungoaded by tormenting reflections, we may bow down our necks, with all the stupid serenity of servitude, to any drudgery, which our lords and masters shall please to command.

When the charges of the "administration of justice," the "support of civil government," and the "expenses of defending, protecting and securing" us, are provided for, I should be glad to know, upon *what occasions* the crown will ever call our assemblies together? Some few of them may meet of their own accord, by virtue of their charters. But what will they have to do, when they are met? To what shadows will they be reduced? The men, whose deliberations heretofore had an influence on every matter relating to the *liberty* and *happiness* of themselves and their constituents, and whose authority in domestic affairs at least, might well be compared to that of *Roman* senators, will *now* find their deliberations of no more consequence, than those of *constables.* They may *perhaps* be allowed to make laws *for the yoking of hogs,* or *pounding of stray cattle.* Their influence will hardly be permitted to extend *so high,* as the *keeping roads in repair,* as *that business* may more properly be executed by those who receive the public cash.

One most memorable example in history is so applicable to the point now insisted on, that it will form a just conclusion of the observations that have been made.

Spain was once *free.* Their *cortes* resembled our parliaments. No *money* could be raised on the subject, *without their consent.* One of their Kings having received a grant from them, to maintain a war against the *Moors,* desired, that if the sum which they had given, should not be sufficient, he might be allowed, *for that emergency only,* to raise more money *without assembling the Cortes.* The request was violently opposed by the best and wisest men in the assembly. It was, however, complied with by the votes of a majority; and this single concession was a PRECEDENT for other concessions of the like kind, until at last the crown obtained a general power of raising money, in cases of necessity. From that period the *Cortes* ceased to be *useful*—the *people* ceased to be *free.*

Venienti occurrite morbo.

Oppose a disease at its beginning.

A Farmer

LETTER X

My dear Countrymen,

The consequences, mentioned in the last letter, will not be the utmost limits of our *misery* and *infamy,* if the late act is acknowledged to be binding upon us. We feel too sensibly, that *any ministerial measures** relating to these colonies, are soon carried successfully through the parliament. Certain prejudices operate there so strongly against us, that it may be justly questioned, whether *all* the provinces united, will ever be able effectually to call to an account before the parliament, any minister who shall abuse the power by the late act given to the crown in *America.* He may divide the spoils torn from us in what manner he pleases, *and we shall have no way of making him responsible.* If he should order, that every *governor* shall have a yearly salary of 5,000£ sterling; every *chief justice* of 3,000£; every inferior officer in proportion; and should then reward the most profligate, ignorant, or needy dependents on himself or his friends, with places of the greatest trust, because they were of the greatest profit, this would be called an arrangement in consequence of the "adequate provision for defraying the charge of the administration of justice, and the support of the civil government": And if the taxes should prove at any time insufficient to answer all the expenses of the numberless offices, which ministers may please to create, surely the members of the house of commons will be so "*modest,*" as not to "contradict a minister" who shall tell them, it is become necessary to lay a new tax upon the colonies, for the laudable purposes of defraying the charges of the "administration of justice, and support of civil government"

* "The gentleman must not wonder he was not contradicted, when, as *minister,* he asserted the right of parliament to tax *America.* I know not how it is, but there is a MODESTY in this house, *which does not choose to contradict a minister.* I wish gentlemen would get the better of this *modesty.* IF THEY DO NOT, PERHAPS THE COLLECTIVE BODY MAY BEGIN TO ABATE OF ITS RESPECT FOR THE REPRESENTATIVE." (*Mr.* Pitt's *Speech*)

among them. Thus, in fact, we shall be taxed by ministers.* In short, it will be in their power to settle upon us any CIVIL, ECCLESIASTICAL, or MILITARY establishment, which they choose.

We may perceive, by the example of *Ireland,* how eager ministers are to seize upon any settled revenue, and apply it in supporting their own power. Happy are the men, and *happy the people who grow wise by the misfortunes of others.* Earnestly, my dear countrymen, do I beseech the author of all good gifts, that you may grow wise in this manner; and if I may be allowed to take such a liberty, I beg leave to recommend to you in general, as the best method of attaining this wisdom, diligently to study the histories of other countries. You will there find all the arts, that can possibly be practiced by cunning rulers, or false patriots among yourselves, so fully delineated, that, changing names, the account would serve for your own times.

It is pretty well known on this continent, that *Ireland* has, with a regular consistency of injustice, been cruelly treated by ministers in the article of *pensions;* but there are some alarming circumstances relating to that subject, which I wish to have better known among us.

†The revenue of the crown there arises principally from the

* "Within this act (*statute de tallagio non concedendo*) are all *new* offices erected with *new* fees, or *old* offices with *new* fees, for that is a tallage put upon the subject, which cannot be done without common assent by act of parliament. And this does notably appear by a petition in parliament in anno 13 H. IV. where the commons complain, that an office was erected for measureage of cloths and canvas, with a new fee for the same, by color of the king's letters patents, and pray that these letters patents may be revoked, for that the king could erect no offices with new fees to be taken of the people, who may not so be charged but by parliament." (2d Inst. p. 533)

† An enquiry into the legality of pensions on the *Irish* establishment, by *Alexander M'Aulay,* Esq.; one of the King's council, etc.

Mr. M'Aulay concludes his piece in the following beautiful manner. "If any *pensions* have been obtained on that establishment, to SERVE THE CORRUPT PURPOSES OF AMBITIOUS MEN—If his Majesty's revenues of *Ireland* have been employed in pensions, TO DEBAUCH HIS MAJESTY'S SUBJECTS of both kingdoms—If the treasure of *Ireland* has been expended in pensions, FOR CORRUPTING MEN OF THAT KINGDOM TO BETRAY THEIR COUNTRY; and men of the neighboring kingdom, to betray both—If *Irish* pensions have been procured, TO SUPPORT GAMESTERS AND GAMING-HOUSES; promoting a vice which threatens national ruin—If pensions have been purloined out of the national treasure of *Ireland,* under the MASK OF SALARIES ANNEXED TO PUBLIC OFFICES, USELESS TO THE NATION; newly invented, FOR THE PURPOSES OF CORRUPTION—If Ireland,

Excise granted "*for pay of the army, and defraying other* PUBLIC *charges, in defense and preservation of the kingdom*"—from the hearth money granted—as a "PUBLIC *revenue,* for PUBLIC *charges and expenses.*" There are some other branches of the revenue, concerning which there is not any express appropriation of them for PUBLIC *service,* but which were plainly *so intended.*

Of these branches of the revenue the crown is only *trustee* for the public. They are unalienable. They are inapplicable to any other purposes, but those for which they were established; and therefore are not *legally* chargeable with pensions.

There is another kind of revenue, which is a private revenue. This is not limited to any public uses; but the crown has the same property in it, that any person has in his estate. This does not amount, at the most to *Fifteen Thousand Pounds* a year, probably not to *Seven,* and is the only revenue, that can be *legally* charged with pensions.

If ministers were accustomed to regard the rights or happiness of the people, the pensions in *Ireland* would not exceed the sum just mentioned: But long since have they exceeded that limit; and in *December* 1765, a motion was made in the house of commons in that kingdom, to address his Majesty on the great increase of pensions on the *Irish* establishment, amounting to the sum of 158,685£—in the last two years.

Attempts have been made to gloss over these gross encroachments, by this specious argument—"That expending a competent part of the PUBLIC REVENUE in pensions, from a principle of

---

just beginning to recover from the devastations of massacre and rebellion, be obstructed in the progress of her cure, BY SWARMS OF PENSIONARY VULTURES PREYING ON HER VITALS—If, by squandering the national substance of *Ireland,* in a LICENTIOUS, UNBOUNDED PROFUSION OF PENSIONS, instead of employing it in nourishing and improving her infant *agriculture, trade* and *manufactures,* or in *enlightening* and *reforming* her *poor, ignorant, deluded, miserable natives* (by nature most amiable, most valuable, most worthy of public attention)—If, *by such abuse of the national substance, sloth* and *nastiness, cold* and *hunger, nakedness* and *wretchedness, popery, depopulation* and *barbarism,* still maintain their ground; *still deform a country, abounding with all the riches of nature,* yet hitherto destined to beggary—IF SUCH PENSIONS be found on the *Irish* establishment; let such be cut off: And let the perfidious advisers be branded with indelible characters of public infamy; adequate, if possible, to the dishonor of their crime."

charity or generosity, adds to the dignity of the crown; and is *therefore* useful to the PUBLIC." To give this argument any weight, it must appear, that the pensions proceed from "*charity* or *generosity* only"—and that it "adds to the dignity of the crown," *to act directly contrary to law.*

From this conduct towards *Ireland,* in open violation of law, we may easily foresee what *we* may expect, when a minister will have the *whole revenue* of *America* in his own hands, to be disposed of at his own pleasure: For *all* the monies raised by the late act are to be "*applied* by virtue of warrants under the sign manual, counter-signed by the high treasurer, or any three of the commissioners of the treasury." The "RESIDUE" indeed is to be "paid into the receipt of the exchequer, and to be disposed of by parliament." So that a minister will have nothing to do, but to take care, that there shall be no "residue," and he is superior to all control.

Besides the burden of *pensions* in *Ireland,* which have enormously increased within these few years, almost all the *offices* in that poor kingdom, have been, since the commencement of the present century, and now are bestowed upon *strangers.* For tho' the merit of persons born there, justly raises them to places of high trust when they go abroad, as all *Europe* can witness, yet he is an uncommonly lucky *Irishman,* who can get a good post *in his* NATIVE *country.*

When I consider the manner* in which that island has been

* In *Charles* the second's time, the house of commons, influenced by some factious demagogues, were resolved to prohibit the importation of *Irish* cattle into *England.* Among other arguments in favor of *Ireland* it was insisted—"That by cutting off almost entirely the trade between the kingdoms, ALL THE NATURAL BANDS OF UNION WERE DISSOLVED, and nothing remained to keep the *Irish* in their duty, but *force* and *violence.*"

"The king (says Mr. *Hume,* in his history of *England*) was so convinced of the justness of these reasons, that he used all his interest to oppose the bill, and he openly declared, that he could not give his assent to it with a safe conscience. But the commons were resolute in their purpose"—"And the spirit of TYRANNY, *of which* NATIONS *are as susceptible* as INDIVIDUALS, had animated the *English* extremely TO EXERT THEIR SUPERIORITY *over their dependent state.* No affair could be conducted with greater violence than this by the commons. They even went so far in the preamble of the bill, as to declare the importation of *Irish* cattle to be a NUISANCE. By this expression they gave scope to their *passion,* and at the same time *barred the king's prerogative,* by which he might think himself entitled to dispense with a law, so FULL OF INJUSTICE

uniformly depressed for so many years past, with this pernicious particularity of their parliament continuing *as long as the crown pleases*,* I am astonished to observe such a love of liberty still animating that LOYAL and GENEROUS nation; and nothing can raise higher my idea of the INTEGRITY and PUBLIC SPIRIT† OF a people, who have preserved the sacred fire of freedom from being extinguished, tho' the altar on which it burnt, has been overturned.

AND BAD POLICY. The lords expunged the word, but as the king was sensible that no supply would be given by the commons, unless they were gratified in all their PREJUDICES, he was obliged both to empty his interest with the peers, to make the bill pass, and to give the royal assent to it. He could not, however, forbear expressing his displeasure at the jealousy entertained against him, and at the intention which the commons discovered, of retrenching his prerogative.

THIS LAW BROUGHT GREAT DISTRESS FOR SOME TIME UPON IRELAND, BUT IT HAS OCCASIONED THEIR APPLYING WITH GREATER INDUSTRY TO MANUFACTURES, AND HAS PROVED IN THE ISSUE BENEFICIAL TO THAT KINGDOM."

Perhaps the *same reason* occasioned the "barring the king's prerogative" in the late act suspending the legislation of *New York*.

This we may be assured of, that WE ARE as dear to his *Majesty*, as the people of *Great Britain* are. We are his *subjects* as they, and as *faithful subjects;* and his Majesty has given too many, too constant proofs of his piety and virtue, for any man to think it possible, that such a *prince* can make any unjust distinction between *such subjects*. It makes no difference to his Majesty, whether supplies are raised in *Great Britain*, or *America;* but it makes *some* difference to the commons of that kingdom.

To speak plainly, as becomes an honest man on such important occasions, all our misfortunes are owing to a LUST OF POWER in men of *abilities* and *influence*. This prompts them to seek POPULARITY by *expedients* profitable to themselves, though ever so destructive to their country.

Such is the accursed nature of lawless ambition, and yet—What heart but melts at the thought!—Such false, detestable PATRIOTS, in *every state*, have led their blind, confiding country, shouting their applauses, into the jaws of *shame* and *ruin*. May the wisdom and goodness of the people of *Great Britain*, save them from the usual fate of nations.

MENTEM MORTALIA TANGUNT.

* The last *Irish* parliament continued 33 years, during all the late King's reign. The present parliament there has continued from the beginning of this reign, and probably will continue till this reign ends.

† I am informed, that within these few years, a petition was presented to the house of commons, setting forth, "that herrings were imported into *Ireland* from some foreign parts of the north so cheap, as to discourage the *British* herring fishery, and therefore praying that some remedy might be applied in that behalf by parliament."

That upon this petition, the house came to a resolution, to impose a duty of Two Shillings sterling on every barrel of foreign herrings imported into *Ireland;* but afterwards

In the same manner shall we unquestionably be treated, as soon as the late taxes laid upon us, shall make posts in the "government," and the "administration of justice" *here,* worth the attention of persons of influence in *Great Britain.* We know enough already to satisfy us of this truth. But this will not be the worst part of our case.

The *principals,* in all great offices, will reside in *England,* making some paltry allowance to deputies for doing the business *here.* Let any consider what an exhausting drain this must be upon us, when ministers are possessed of the power of creating what posts they please, and of affixing to such posts what salaries they please, and he must be convinced how destructive the late act will be. The injured kingdom lately mentioned, can tell us the mischiefs of ABSENTEES; and we may perceive already the same disposition taking place with us. The government of *New York* has been exercised by a deputy. That of *Virginia* is now held so; and we know of a number of secretaryships, collectorships, and other offices, held in the same manner.

True it is, that if the people of *Great Britain* were not too much blinded by the passions, that have been artfully excited in their breasts, against their dutiful children the colonists, these considerations would be nearly as alarming to them as to us. The influence of the crown was thought by wise men, many years ago, too great, by reason of the multitude of pensions and places bestowed by it. These have been vastly increased since,* and perhaps it would be no difficult matter to prove that the people have decreased.

---

dropt the affair, FOR FEAR OF ENGAGING IN A DISPUTE WITH IRELAND ABOUT THE RIGHT OF TAXING HER.

So much higher was the opinion, which the house entertained of the spirit of *Ireland,* than of that of these colonies.

I find, in the last *English* papers, that the resolution and firmness with which the people of *Ireland* have lately asserted their freedom, have been so alarming in *Great Britain,* that the Lord Lieutenant, in his speech on the 20th of last *October,* "recommended to that parliament, that such provision may be made for securing the judges in the enjoyment of their offices and appointments, DURING THEIR GOOD BEHAVIOR, as shall be thought most expedient."

What an important concession is thus obtained, by making demands becoming freemen, with a courage and perseverance becoming Freemen!

* One of the reasons urged by that great and honest statesman, *Sir William Temple,* to *Charles* the Second, in his famous remonstrance, to dissuade him from aiming at arbitrary power, was that the King "had few offices to bestow." (*Hume's* Hist. of *England*)

Surely therefore, those who wish the welfare of their country, ought seriously to reflect, what may be the consequence of such a new creation of offices, in the disposal of the crown. The *army,* the *administration of justice,* and the *civil government* here, with such salaries as the crown shall please to annex, will extend *ministerial influence* as much beyond its former bounds, as the late war did the *British* dominions.

But whatever the people of *Great Britain* may think on this occasion, I hope the people of these colonies will unanimously join in this sentiment, that the late act of parliament is injurious to their liberty, and that this sentiment will unite them in a firm opposition to it, in the same manner as the dread of the *Stamp Act* did.

Some persons may imagine the sums to be raised by it, are but small, and therefore may be inclined to acquiesce under it. A conduct more dangerous to freedom, as before has been observed, can never be adopted. Nothing is wanted at home but a PRECEDENT,* the force of which shall be established, by the tacit submission of the colonies. With what zeal was the statute erecting the post office, and another relating to the recovery of debts in *America,* urged and tor-

---

"Tho' the wings of prerogative have been clipped, the influence of the crown is greater than ever it was in any period of our history. For when we consider in how many boroughs the government has the votes at command; when we consider the vast body of persons employed in the collection of the revenue, in every part of the kingdom, the inconceivable number of placemen, and candidates for places in the customs, in the excise, in the post-office, in the dock-yards, in the ordnance, in the salt-office, in the stamps, in the navy and victualling offices, and in a variety of other departments; when we consider again the extensive influence of the money corporations, subscription jobbers and contractors, the endless dependencies created by the obligations conferred on the bulk of the gentlemen's families throughout the kingdom, who have relations preferred in our navy and numerous standing army; when I say, we consider how wide, how binding a dependence on the crown is created by the above enumerated particulars, and the great, the enormous weight and influence which the crown derives from this extensive dependence upon its favor and power, any lord in waiting, any lord of the bed-chamber, any man may be appointed minister." A doctrine to this effect is said to have been the advice of L——H——. (*Late News Paper*)

* Here may be observed, that when any ancient law or custom of parliament is broken, and the crown possessed of a *precedent,* how *difficult a thing it is to restore the subject again to his* FORMER FREEDOM *and* SAFETY." (2d *Coke's Inst.* p. 529)

"It is not almost credible to *foresee,* when any maxim or *fundamental law* of this realm is altered (as elsewhere hath been observed) what *dangerous inconveniences* do follow." (4th *Coke's Inst.* p. 41)

tured, as *precedents* in support of the *Stamp Act,* tho' wholly inapplicable. If the parliament succeeds in this attempt, other statutes will impose other duties. Instead of taxing ourselves, as we have been accustomed to do, from the first settlement of these provinces, all our usual taxes will be converted into parliamentary taxes on our importations; and thus the parliament will levy upon us such sums of money as they choose to take, *without any other* LIMITATION, *than their* PLEASURE.

We know how much labor and care have been bestowed by these colonies, in laying taxes in such a manner, that they should be most *easy* to the people, by being laid on the proper articles; most *equal,* by being proportioned to every man's circumstances; and *cheapest,* by the method directed for collecting them.

But *parliamentary taxes* will be laid on us, without any consideration, whether there is any easier mode. The *only point* regarded will be, the *certainty of levying the taxes,* and not the convenience of the people on whom they are to be levied; and therefore all statutes on this head will be such as will be most likely, according to the favorite phrase, "*to execute themselves.*"

Taxes in every free state have been, and ought to be, as exactly *proportioned as is possible to the abilities of those who are to pay them.* They cannot otherwise be *just.* Even a *Hottentot* would comprehend the unreasonableness of making a poor man pay as much for "defending" the property of a rich man, as the rich man pays himself.

Let any person look into the late act of parliament, and he will immediately perceive, that the immense estates of Lord *Fairfax,* Lord *Baltimore,* and our *Proprietaries,** which are among his Majesty's other "DOMINIONS" to be "defended, protected and secured" by the act, will not pay a *single farthing* for the duties thereby imposed, except Lord *Fairfax* wants some of his windows glazed; Lord *Baltimore* and our *Proprietaries* are quite secure, as they live in *England.*

* *Maryland* and *Pennsylvania* have been engaged in the warmest disputes, in order to obtain an equal and just taxation of their Proprietors' estates: But this late act of parliament does more for those Proprietors, than they themselves would venture to demand. It totally exempts them from taxation—tho' their vast estates are to be "secured" by the taxes of other people.

I mention these particular cases, as striking instances how far the late act is a deviation from that *principle of justice,* which has so constantly distinguished our own laws on this continent, and ought to be regarded in all laws.

The third consideration with our continental assemblies in laying taxes, has been the *method* of collecting them. This has been done by a few officers, with moderate allowances, under the inspection of the respective assemblies. *No more was raised from the subject,* than was used for the intended purposes. But by the late act, a minister may appoint *as many officers as he pleases* for collecting the taxes; may assign them *what salaries he thinks* "adequate"; and they are subject to *no inspection but his own.*

In short, if the late act of parliament takes effect, these colonies must dwindle down into "COMMON CORPORATIONS," as their enemies, in the debates concerning the repeal of the *Stamp Act, strenuously insisted they were;* and it seems not improbable that some future historian may thus record our fall.

"The eighth year of this reign was distinguished by a *very memorable event,* the *American* colonies then submitting, for the FIRST time, to be *taxed* by the *British* parliament. An attempt of this kind had been made about two years before, but was defeated by the vigorous exertions of the several provinces, in defense of their liberties. Their behavior on that occasion rendered their name very celebrated *for a short time* all over *Europe;* all states being extremely attentive to the dispute between *Great Britain,* and so considerable a part of her dominions. For as she was thought to be grown too powerful, but the successful conclusion of the late war she had been engaged in, it was hoped by many, that as it had happened before to other kingdoms, civil discords would afford opportunities of revenging all the injuries supposed to be received from her. However, the cause of dissension was removed, by a repeal of the statute that had given offense. This affair rendered the SUBMISSIVE CONDUCT of the colonies so soon after, the more extraordinary; there being *no difference* between the mode of taxation which they opposed, and that to which they submitted, but this, that by the first, they were to be continually *reminded* that they *were taxed,* by certain marks *stamped* on every piece of paper or parchment they used. The authors of *that statute* triumphed greatly on this conduct of the colonies, and insisted, that if the people of *Great Britain* had persisted in enforcing it, the *Americans* would have been, in a few months, *so fatigued with the efforts of patriotism,* that they would have yielded obedience.

"Certain it is, that though they had before their eyes *so many illustrious examples* in their mother country, of the *constant* success attending *firmness* and *perseverance,* in opposition to dangerous encroachments on liberty, yet they quietly gave up a point of the LAST IMPORTANCE. From thence the decline of their freedom began, and its decay was extremely rapid; for *as money* was always raised upon them by the parliament, their *assemblies* grew immediately *useless,* and in a short time *contemptible:* And in less than one hundred years, the people sunk down into that *tameness* and *supineness* of spirit, by which they still continue to be distinguished."

Et majores vestros & posteros cogitate.

Remember your ancestors and your posterity.

A Farmer

LETTER XI

My dear Countrymen,

I have several times, in the course of these letters, mentioned the late act of parliament, as being the *foundation* of future measures injurious to these colonies; and the belief of this truth I wish to prevail, because I think it necessary to our safety.

A perpetual *jealousy,* respecting liberty, is absolutely requisite in all free states. The very texture of their constitution, in *mixed* governments, demands it. For the *cautions* with which power is distributed among the several orders, *imply,* that *each* has that share which is proper for the general welfare, and therefore that any further acquisition must be pernicious. *Machiavel* employs a whole chapter in his discourses,* to prove that a state, to be long lived, must be frequently corrected, and reduced to its first principles. But of all states that have existed, there never was any, in which this jealousy could be more proper than in these colonies. For the government here is not only *mixed,* but *dependent,* which circumstance occasions *a peculiarity in its form,* of a very delicate nature.

Two reasons induce me to desire, that this spirit of apprehension may be always kept up among us, in its utmost vigilance. The first is this—that as the happiness of these provinces indubitably consists in their connection with *Great Britain,* any separation between them is less likely to be occasioned by civil discords, if every disgusting measure is opposed singly, and *while it is new:* For in this manner of proceeding, every such measure is most likely to be rectified. On the other hand, oppressions and dissatisfactions being permitted to accumulate—*if ever* the governed throw off the load, *they will do more.* A people does not reform with moderation. The rights of the subject therefore cannot be *too often* considered, explained or asserted: And whoever attempts to do this, shows himself, whatever may be the rash and peevish reflections of pretended wisdom, and pretended duty, a friend to *those* who injudiciously exercise their power, as well as to *them,* over whom it is so exercised.

Had all the points of prerogative claimed by *Charles* the First, been separately contested and settled in preceding reigns, his fate would in all probability have been very different; and the people would have been content with that liberty which is compatible with regal authority. But he thought, it would be as dangerous for him to give up the powers which at any time had been by usurpation exercised by the crown, as those that were legally vested in it.† This produced

* *Machiavel's Discourses—Book* 3. *Chap.* I.

† The author is sensible that this is putting the gentlest construction on *Charles's* conduct; and that is one reason why he chooses it. Allowances ought to be made for the errors

an equal excess on the part of the people. For when their passions were excited by *multiplied* grievances, they thought it would be as dangerous for them to allow the powers that were legally vested in the crown, as those which at any time had been by usurpation exercised by it. Acts, that might *by themselves* have been upon many considerations excused or extenuated, derived a contagious malignancy and odium from other acts, with which they were connected. They were not regarded according to the simple force of each, but as parts of a system of oppression. Every one therefore, however small in itself, became alarming, as an additional evidence of tyrannical designs. It was in vain for prudent and moderate men to insist, that there was no necessity to abolish royalty. Nothing less than the utter destruction of monarchy, could satisfy those who *had* suffered, and thought they had reason to believe, they always *should* suffer under it.

The consequences of these mutual distrusts are well known: But there is no other people mentioned in history, that I recollect, who have been so constantly watchful of their liberty, and so successful in their struggles for it, as the *English*. This consideration leads me to the second reason, why I "desire that the spirit of apprehension may be always kept among us in its utmost vigilance."

The first principles of government are to be looked for in human nature. Some of the best writers have asserted, and it seems with good reason, that "government is founded on *opinion*."*

---

of those men, who are acknowledged to have been possessed of many virtues. The education of this unhappy prince, and his confidence in men not so good or wise as himself, had probably *filled* him with mistaken notions of his own authority, and of the consequences that would attend concessions of any kind to a people, who were represented to him, as aiming at too much power.

* "Opinion is of two kinds, *viz.*, *opinion* of INTEREST, and *opinion* of RIGHT. By *opinion* of *interest,* I chiefly understand, *the sense of the public advantage which is reaped from government;* together with the persuasion, that the particular government which is established, *is equally advantageous* with any other, *that could be easily settled.*"

"*Right* is of two kinds, *right* to *power,* and *right* to *property.* What prevalence *opinion* of the first kind has over mankind, may easily be understood, by observing the attachment which all nations have to their ancient government, and even to those names which have had the sanction of antiquity. *Antiquity always begets the opinion of right*"—"It is sufficiently understood, that the *opinion of right to property,* is of the greatest moment in all matters of government." (*Hume's Essays*)

Custom undoubtedly has a mighty force in producing *opinion,* and reigns in nothing more arbitrarily than in public affairs. It gradually reconciles us to objects even of dread and detestation; and I cannot but think these lines of Mr. *Pope* as applicable to vice in *politics,* as to vice in *ethics*—

Vice is a monster of so horrid mien,
As to be hated, needs but to be seen;
Yet *seen too oft,* familiar with her face,
We first *endure,* then *pity,* then *embrace.*

When an act injurious to freedom has been *once* done, and the people *bear* it, the *repetition* of it is most likely to meet with submission. For as the *mischief* of the one was found to be tolerable, they will hope that of the second will prove so too; and they will not regard the *infamy* of the last, because they are stained with that of the first.

Indeed nations, in general, are not apt to *think* until they *feel;* and therefore nations in general have lost their liberty: For as violations of the rights of the *governed,* are commonly not only *specious,** but *small* at the beginning, they spread over the multitude in such a manner, as to touch individuals but slightly.† Thus they are disregarded. The power or profit that arises from these violations, *centering in few persons,* is to them considerable. For this reason the *governors* having in view their particular purposes, successfully preserve a uniformity of conduct for attaining them. They regularly increase the first injuries, till at length the inattentive people are compelled to perceive

* *Omnia mala exempla ex bonis initiis orta sunt.* (SALLUST. *Bell. Cat.* S. 50)

† "The *republic* is always *attacked* with greater vigor, than it is *defended:* For the *audacious* and *profligate,* prompted by their natural enmity to it, are *easily impelled* to act by the *least nod* of their *leaders:* Whereas the HONEST, I know not why, are generally *slow* and *unwilling* to stir; and *neglecting* always the BEGINNINGS *of things,* are *never roused* to exert themselves, but by the *last necessity:* So that through IRRESOLUTION and DELAY, when they would be glad to compound at last for the QUIET, at the expense even of their HONOR, they *commonly lose them* BOTH." (CICERO'S *Orat. for* SEXTIUS)

Such were the sentiments of this great and excellent man, whose vast abilities, and the calamities of his country during this time enabled him, by mournful experience, to form a just judgment on the conduct of the friends and enemies of liberty.

the heaviness of their burdens—They begin to complain and inquire—but too late. They find their oppressors so strengthened by success, and themselves so entangled in examples of express authority on the part of their rulers, and of tacit recognition on their own part, that they are quite confounded: For millions entertain no other idea of the *legality* of power, than that it is founded on the exercise of power. They voluntarily fasten their chains, by adopting a pusillanimous *opinion,* "that there will be too much *danger* in attempting a remedy"—or another *opinion* no less fatal—"that the government has a *right* to treat them as it does." They then seek a wretched relief for their minds, by persuading themselves, that to yield their *obedience,* is to discharge their *duty.* The deplorable *poverty of spirit,* that prostrates all the dignity bestowed by divine providence on our nature—*of course succeeds.*

From these reflections I conclude, that every free state should incessantly watch, and instantly take alarm on any addition being made to the power exercised over them. Innumerable instances might be produced to show, from what slight beginnings the most extensive consequences have flowed: But I shall select two only from the history of England.

Henry the Seventh was the *first* monarch of that kingdom, who established a STANDING BODY OF ARMED MEN. This was a band of *fifty* archers, called yeomen of the guard: And this institution, notwithstanding the smallness of the number, was, to prevent discontent, "disguised under pretence of majesty and grandeur."* In 1684 the standing forces were so much augmented, that *Rapin* says—"The king, in order to make his people *fully sensible of their new slavery,* affected to muster his troops, which amounted to 4000 well armed and disciplined men." I think our army, at this time, consists of more than *seventy* regiments.

The method of taxing by EXCISE was first introduced amid the convulsions of the civil wars. Extreme necessity was pretended for it, and its short continuance promised. After the restoration, an excise upon *beer, ale* and *other liquors,* was granted to the king,† one

* *Rapin's* History of *England.*

† *Char.* II. Chap. 23 and 24.

half in fee, the other for life, as an equivalent for the *court of wards.* Upon *James* the Second's accession, the parliament gave him the first *excise,* with an additional duty on *wine, tobacco,* and some *other* things.* Since the revolution it has been extended to salt, candles, leather, hides, hops, soap, paper, pasteboards, mill-boards, scale-boards, vellum, parchment, starch, silks, calicos, linens, stuffs, printed, stained, etc. wire, wrought plate, coffee, tea, chocolate, etc.

Thus a *standing army* and *excise* have, from their first slender origins, tho' always *hated,* always *feared,* always *opposed,* at length swelled up to their vast present bulk.

These facts are sufficient to support what I have said. It is true, that all the mischiefs apprehended by our ancestors from a *standing army* and *excise,* have not *yet happened:* But it does not follow from this, that they *will not happen.* The inside of a house may catch fire, and the most valuable apartments be ruined, before the flames burst out. The question in these cases is not, what evil *has actually attended* particular measures—but, what evil, in the nature of things, *is likely to attend* them. Certain circumstances may for some time delay effects, that *were reasonably expected,* and that *must ensue.* There was a long period, after the *Romans* had prorogued his command to Q. *Publilius Philo,* before *that example* destroyed their liberty.† All our kings, from the revolution to the present reign, have been *foreigners.* Their *ministers* generally continued but a short time in authority and they themselves were *mild* and *virtuous* princes.‡

A bold, *ambitious* prince, possessed of *great abilities,* firmly *fixed* in his throne *by descent,* served by *ministers like* himself, and rendered

* I *James* II. Chap. 1 and 4.

† In the year of the city 428, "*Duo singularia haec ei viro primum contigere; prorogatio imperii non ante in ullo facta, et acto honore triumphus.*" (*Liv. B.S. Chap.* 23. 26)

"Had the rest of the *Roman* citizens imitated the example of L. *Quintius,* who refused to have his consulship continued to him, they have never admitted that custom of proroguing of magistrates, and then the prolongation of their commands in the army had never been introduced, *which very thing was at length the ruin of that commonwealth.*" (*Machiavel's Discourses, B. 3. Chap. 24)*

‡ I don't know but it may be said, with a good deal of reason, that a quick rotation of ministers is very desirable in *Great Britain.* A minister there has a vast store of materials to work with. *Long administrations* are rather favorable to the reputation of a people abroad, than to their *liberty.*

either *venerable* or *terrible* by the *glory of his successes,* may execute what his predecessors did not dare to attempt. *Henry* the Fourth tottered in his seat during his whole reign. *Henry* the Fifth drew the strength of that kingdom into *France,* to carry on his wars there, and left the *commons* at home, *protesting,* "that the people were not bound to serve out of the realm."

It is true, that a strong spirit of liberty subsists at present in *Great Britain,* but what reliance is to be placed in the *temper* of a people, when the prince is possessed of an unconstitutional power, our own history can sufficiently inform us. When *Charles* the Second had strengthened himself by the return of the garrison of *Tangier,* "*England* (says *Rapin*) saw on a sudden an *amazing revolution;* saw herself *stripped of all her rights and privileges,* excepting such as the king should vouchsafe to grant her: And what is *more astonishing,* the *English* themselves *delivered up* these very rights and privileges to *Charles* the Second, which they had so *passionately,* and, if I may say it, *furiously* defended against the designs of *Charles* the First." This happened only *thirty-six* years after this last prince had been beheaded.

Some persons are of opinion, that liberty is not violated, but by such *open* acts of force; but they seem to be greatly mistaken. I could mention a period within these forty years, when almost as great a change of disposition was produced by the SECRET measures of a *long* administration, as by *Charles's* violence. Liberty, perhaps, is never exposed to so much danger, as when the people believe there is the least; for it may be subverted, and yet they not think so.

Public disgusting acts are seldom practised by the ambitious, at the beginning of their designs. Such conduct *silences* and *discourages* the weak, and the wicked, who would otherwise have been their *advocates* or *accomplices.* It is of great consequence, to allow those who, upon any account, are inclined to favor them, something specious to say in their defense. Their power may be fully established, tho' it would not be safe for them to do *whatever they please.* For there are things, which, at some times, even *slaves* will not bear. *Julius Caesar,* and *Oliver Cromwell,* did not dare to assume the title of *king.* The *Grand Seignor* dares not lay a *new tax.* The king of *France* dares not be a *protestant.* Certain popular points may be left untouched, and yet freedom be extinguished. The commonalty of Venice imagine themselves free, because they are permitted to do what they ought not. But I quit a subject, that would lead me too far from my purpose.

By the late act of parliament, taxes are to be levied upon us, for "defraying the charge of the *administration of justice*—the support of *civil government*—and the expenses of defending his Majesty's dominions in *America*."

If any man doubts what ought to be the conduct of these colonies on this occasion, I would ask him these questions.

Has not the parliament *expressly* AVOWED their INTENTION of raising money from US FOR CERTAIN PURPOSES? Is not this scheme *popular* in *Great Britain?* Will the taxes, imposed by the late act, *answer those purposes?* If it will, must it not take an immense sum from us? If it will not, *is it to be expected*, that the parliament will not *fully execute* their INTENTION when it is *pleasing at home*, and *not opposed here?* Must not this be done by imposing NEW *taxes?* Will not every addition, thus made to our taxes, be an addition to the power of the *British* legislature, by *increasing the number of officers* employed in the collection? Will not every additional tax therefore render it *more difficult* to abrogate any of them? When a branch of revenue is once established, does it not appear to many people *invidious* and *undutiful*, to attempt to abolish it? If taxes, sufficient to *accomplish the* INTENTION of the parliament, are imposed by the parliament, *what taxes will remain* to be imposed by our assemblies? If *no material taxes remain* to be imposed by them, what must become of *them*, and the *people* they represent?

"If any person considers these things, and yet thinks our liberties are in no danger, I wonder at that person's security."*

One other argument is to be added, which, by itself, I hope, will be sufficient to convince the most incredulous man on this continent, that the late act of parliament is *only* designed to be a PRECEDENT, whereon the future vassalage of these colonies may be established.

Every duty thereby laid on articles of *British* manufacture, is

* *Demosthenes's* 2d Philippic.

laid on some commodity, upon the exportation of which from *Great Britain,* a *drawback* is payable. Those *drawbacks,* in most of the articles, are *exactly double* to the *duties* given by the late act. The parliament therefore might, in *half a dozen lines,* have raised MUCH MORE MONEY, only by *stopping the drawbacks* in the hands of the officers at home, on exportation to these colonies, than by this solemn imposition of taxes upon us, to be collected here. Probably, the artful contrivers of this act formed it in this manner, in order to reserve to themselves, in case of any objections being made to it, this specious pretence—"that the drawbacks are gifts to the colonies, and that the late act only lessens those gifts." But the truth is, that the drawbacks are intended for the encouragement and promotion of *British* manufactures and commerce, and are allowed on exportation to *any foreign parts,* as well as on exportation to these provinces. Besides, care has been taken to slide into the act, some articles on which there are no drawbacks. However, the *whole duties* laid by the late act on *all* the articles therein specified are *so small,* that they will not amount to *as much as* the *drawbacks* which are allowed on *part* of them only. If therefore, *the sum to be obtained by the late act,* had been the *sole object* in forming it, there would not have been any occasion for "the COMMONS of *Great Britain,* to GIVE and GRANT to his Majesty RATES and DUTIES for *raising a revenue* IN *his Majesty's dominions* in America, for making a more certain and adequate provision for defraying the charges of the administration of justice, the support of civil government, and the expense of defending the said dominions"; nor would there have been any occasion for an expensive board of commissioners,* and all the other new charges to which we are made liable.

* The expense of this board, I am informed, is between Four and Five thousand Pounds Sterling a year. The establishment of officers, for collecting the revenue in *America,* amounted before to Seven Thousand Six Hundred Pounds *per annum;* and yet, says the author of "The regulation of the colonies," "the whole remittance from *all* the taxes in the colonies, at an average of *thirty years,* has not amounted to One Thousand Nine Hundred Pounds a year, and in that sum Seven or Eight Hundred Pounds *per annum* only, have been remitted from *North America.*"

The smallness of the revenue arising from the duties in *America,* demonstrates that they were intended only as REGULATIONS OF TRADE: And can any person be so

Upon the whole, for my part, I regard the late act as an *experiment made of our disposition.* It is a bird sent out over the waters, to discover, whether the waves, that lately agitated this part of the world with such violence, have yet *subsided.* If *this adventurer* gets footing here, we shall quickly find it to be of the kind described by the poet.*

"Infelix vates."

A direful foreteller of future calamities.

A Farmer

LETTER XII

My dear Countrymen,

Some states have lost their liberty by *particular accidents:* But this calamity is generally owing to the *decay of virtue.* A *people* is travelling fast to destruction, when *individuals* consider *their* interests as distinct from *those of the public.* Such notions are fatal to their country, and to themselves. Yet how many are there, so *weak* and *sordid* as to *think* they perform *all the offices of life,* if they earnestly endeavor to increase their own *wealth, power,* and *credit,* without the least regard for the society, under the protection of which they live; who, if they can make an *immediate profit to themselves,* by lending

blind to truth, so dull of apprehension in a matter of unspeakable importance to his country, as to imagine, that the board of commissioners lately established at such a charge, is instituted to assist in collecting One Thousand Nine Hundred Pounds a year, or the trifling duties imposed by the late act? Surely every man on this continent must perceive, that they are established for the care of a NEW SYSTEM OF REVENUE, which is but now begun.

* "Dira caelaeno," etc. *Virgil, Aeneid 3.*

their assistance to those, whose projects plainly tend to the injury of their country, rejoice in their *dexterity,* and believe themselves entitled to the character of *able politicians.* Miserable men! Of whom it is hard to say, whether they ought to be most the objects of *pity* or *contempt:* But whose opinions are certainly as *detestable,* as their practices are *destructive.*

Though I always reflect, with a high pleasure, on the integrity and understanding of my countrymen, which, joined with a pure and humble devotion to the great and gracious author of every blessing they enjoy, will, I hope, ensure to them, and their posterity, all temporal and eternal happiness; yet when I consider, that in every age and country there have been bad men, my heart, at this threatening period, is so full of apprehension, as not to permit me to believe, but that there may be some on this continent, *against whom you ought to be upon your guard*—Men,* who either hold, or expect to hold certain

* It is not intended, by these words, to throw any reflection upon gentlemen, because they are possessed of offices: For many of them are certainly men of virtue, and lovers of their country. But supposed obligations of *gratitude,* and *honor,* may induce them to be silent. Whether these obligations *ought to be* regarded or not, is not so much to be considered by others, in the judgment they form of these gentlemen, as whether they *think they* ought to be regarded. Perhaps, therefore, we shall act in the properest manner towards them, if we neither *reproach* nor *imitate* them. The persons meant in this letter, are the *base spirited wretches,* who may endeavor to *distinguish themselves,* by their sordid zeal in defending and promoting measures, which *they know, beyond all question,* to be *destructive* to the *just rights* and *true interests* of their country. It is scarcely possible to speak of *these men* with any degree of *patience*—It is scarcely possible to speak of them with any degree of *propriety*—For no words can truly describe their *guilt* and *meanness*—But every honest bosom, on their being mentioned, will feel what cannot be *expressed.*

If their wickedness did not blind them, they might perceive along the coast of these colonies, many men, remarkable instances of wrecked ambition, who, after *distinguishing themselves* in the support of the *Stamp Act,* by a courageous contempt of their country, and of justice, have been left to linger out their miserable existence, without a government, collectorship, secretaryship, or any other commission, to console them *as well as it could,* for loss of virtue and reputation—while numberless offices have been bestowed in these colonies on people from *Great Britain,* and new ones are continually invented, to be thus bestowed. As a *few great prizes* are put into a lottery to TEMPT *multitudes to lose, so here* and *there* an *American* has been raised to a good post.

Apparent rari nantes in gurgite vasto.

Mr. *Greenville,* indeed, in order to recommend the *Stamp Act,* had the *unequalled* generosity, to pour down a golden shower of offices upon *Americans;* and yet these *ungrateful* colonies did not thank Mr. *Greenville* for showing his kindness to their countrymen, nor *them* for accepting it. How

advantages, by setting examples of servility to their countrymen. Men, who trained to the employment, or self taught by a natural versatility of genius, serve as decoys for drawing the innocent and unwary into snares. It is not to be doubted but that such men will diligently bestir themselves on this and every like occasion, to spread the infection of their meanness as far as they can. On the plans *they* have adopted, this is *their* course. *This* is the method to recommend themselves to their *patrons.*

From *them* we shall learn, how *pleasant* and *profitable* a thing it is, to be for our SUBMISSIVE behavior *well spoken of* at *St. James's,* or *St. Stephen's;* at *Guildhall,* or the *Royal Exchange.* Specious fallacies will be dressed up with all the arts of delusion, to persuade one colony *to distinguish herself from another,* by unbecoming condescensions, *which will serve the ambitious purposes of great men at home,* and therefore will be thought by them *to entitle their assistants in obtaining them* to considerable rewards.

Our fears will be excited. Our homes will be awakened. It will be insinuated to us, with a plausible affectation of *wisdom* and *concern,* how *prudent* it is to please the *powerful*—how *dangerous* to provoke them—and then comes in the perpetual incantation that freezes up every generous purpose of the soul in cold, inactive expectation—"that if there is any request to be made, compliance will obtain a favorable attention."

Our *vigilance* and our *union* are *success* and *safety.* Our *negligence* and our *division* are *distress* and *death.* They are *worse*—They are *shame* and *slavery.* Let us equally shun the benumbing stillness of *overweening sloth,* and the feverish activity of that *ill informed zeal,*

---

must that great statesman have been surprised, to find, that the unpolished colonies could not be reconciled to *infamy,* to *treachery?* Such a *bountiful* disposition towards us never appeared in any minister before him, and probably never will appear again: For it is evident, that *such a system* of policy is to be established on this continent, as, in a short time, is to render it utterly unnecessary to use the least *art* in order to *conciliate* our approbation of any measures. Some of our countrymen may be employed to *fix* chains upon us, but *they* will never be permitted to *hold* them afterwards. So that the utmost, that any of them can expect, is only a *temporary provision,* that *may* expire in their own time; but which, they may *be assured,* will preclude their children from having any consideration paid to *them.* NATIVES of *America* must sink into total NEGLECT and CONTEMPT, the moment that THEIR COUNTRY loses the constitutional powers she now possesses.

which busies itself in maintaining *little, mean* and *narrow* opinions. Let us, with a truly wise *generosity* and *charity,* banish and discourage all *illiberal distinctions,* which may arise from differences in *situation,* forms of *government,* or modes of *religion.* Let us consider ourselves as MEN—FREEMEN—CHRISTIAN FREEMEN—*separated from the rest of the world, and firmly bound together* by the *same rights, interests* and *dangers.* Let *these* keep our attention inflexibly fixed on the GREAT OBJECTS, which we must CONTINUALLY REGARD, in order to *preserve those rights, to promote those interests,* and to *avert those dangers.*

Let these *truths* be indelibly impressed on our minds—*that* we *cannot be* HAPPY, *without being* FREE—that we cannot be free, *without being secure in our property*—that *we* cannot be secure in our property, *if, without our consent, others may, as by right, take it away*—that *taxes imposed on us by parliament,* do thus take it away—that *duties laid for the sole purpose of raising money,* are taxes—that *attempts* to lay such duties *should be instantly and firmly opposed*—that this opposition can never be effectual, *unless it is the united effort of these provinces*—that therefore BENEVOLENCE *of temper towards each other,* and UNANIMITY *of counsels,* are essential to the welfare of the whole—and lastly, that for this reason, every man among us, who in any manner would encourage either *dissension, dissidence,* or *indifference,* between these colonies, is an enemy to *himself,* and *to his country.*

The belief of these truths, I verily think, my countrymen, is indispensably necessary to your happiness. I beseech you, therefore, "teach them diligently unto your children, and talk of them when you sit in your houses, and when you walk by the way, and when you lie down, and when you rise up."*

What have these colonies to *ask,* while they continue free? Or what have they to *dread,* but insidious attempts to subvert their freedom? *Their prosperity* does not depend on *ministerial favors doled out* to *particular* provinces. *They* form *one* political body, of which *each colony is a member. Their happiness* is founded on *their constitution;* and is to be promoted, by preserving that constitution in unabated

* Deuteronomy 6:7.

vigor, *throughout every part.* A spot, a speck of decay, however small the limb on which it appears, and however remote it may seem from the vitals, should be alarming. We have *all the rights* requisite for our prosperity. The legal authority of *Great Britain* may indeed lay hard restrictions upon us; but, like the spear of *Telephus,* it will cure as well as wound. Her unkindness will instruct and compel us, after some time, to discover, in our *industry* and *frugality,* surprising remedies—*if our rights continue unviolated:* For as long as the *products* of our *labor,* and the *rewards* of our *care, can properly* be called *our own,* so long it will be worth our while to be *industrious* and *frugal.* But if when we plow—sow—reap—gather—and thresh—we find, that we plow—sow—reap—gather—and thresh *for others,* whose PLEASURE is to be the SOLE LIMITATION *how much* they shall *take,* and *how much* they shall *leave,* WHY should we repeat the unprofitable toil? *Horses* and *oxen* are content with *that portion of the fruits of their work,* which their *owners* assign them, in order to keep them strong enough to raise successive crops; but even *these beasts* will not submit to draw for their *masters,* until they are *subdued* by *whips* and *goads.*

Let us take care of our *rights,* and we *therein* take care of *our prosperity.* "SLAVERY IS EVER PRECEDED BY SLEEP."* *Individuals* may be *dependent* on ministers, if they please. STATES SHOULD SCORN IT—and if *you* are not wanting *to yourselves,* you will have a *proper regard* paid *you* by *those,* to whom if you are not *respectable,* you will be *contemptible.* But—if *we have already forgot* the *reasons* that urged us with unexampled unanimity, to exert ourselves two years ago—if *our zeal* for the public good is *worn out* before the *homespun cloths,* which it caused us to have made—if *our resolutions* are *so faint,* as by our present conduct to *condemn* our own late *successful* example—if *we are not affected* by any reverence for the memory of our ancestors, who transmitted to us that freedom in which they had been blessed—if *we are not animated* by any regard for posterity, to whom, by the most sacred obligations, we are bound to deliver down the invaluable inheritance—THEN, indeed, any *minister*—or any *tool* of a minister—or any *creature* of a tool of a

* *Montesquieu's* Spirit of Laws, Book 14, Chap. 13.

minister—or any *lower instrument* of administration,*† if lower there be, is a *personage* whom it may be dangerous to offend.

I shall be extremely sorry, if any man mistakes my meaning in any thing I have said. Officers employed by the crown, are, while according to the laws they conduct themselves, entitled to legal obedience, and sincere respect. These it is a duty to render them; and these no good or prudent person will withhold. But when these officers, through rashness or design, desire to enlarge their authority beyond its due limits, and expect improper concessions to be made to them, from regard for the employments they bear, their attempts should be considered as equal injuries to the crown and people, and should

* "Instrumenta regni." *Tacitus's* Ann. *Book* 12. § 66.

† If any person shall imagine that he discovers, in these letters, the least dislike of the dependence of these colonies on *Great Britain,* I beg that such person will not form any judgment on *particular expressions,* but will consider the *tenor of all the letters taken together.* In that case, I flatter myself, that every unprejudiced reader will be *convinced,* that the true interests of *Great Britain* are as dear to me, as they ought to be to every good subject.

If I am an *Enthusiast* in any thing, it is in my zeal for the *perpetual dependence* of these colonies on their mother country—A dependence founded on *mutual benefits,* the continuance of which can be secured only by *mutual affections.* Therefore it is, that with extreme apprehension I view the smallest seeds of discontent, which are unwarily scattered abroad. *Fifty* or *Sixty* years will make astonishing alterations in these colonies; and this consideration should render it the business of *Great Britain* more and more to cultivate our good dispositions towards her: But the misfortune is, that those *great men,* who wrestling for power at home, think themselves very slightly interested in the prosperity of their country *Fifty or Sixty* years hence, but are deeply concerned in blowing up a popular clamor for supposed *immediate advantages.*

For my part, I regret *Great Britain* as a Bulwark, happily fixed between these colonies and the powerful nations of *Europe.* That kingdom remaining safe, we, under its protection, enjoying peace, may diffuse the blessings of religion, science, and liberty, through remote wilderness. It is therefore incontestably our *duty,* and our interest, to support the strength of *Great Britain.* When confiding in that strength, she begins to forget from whence it arose, it will be an easy thing to show the source. She may readily be reminded of the loud alarm spread among her merchants and tradesmen, by the universal association of these colonies, at the time of the *Stamp Act,* not to import any of her MANUFACTURES.

In the year 1718, the *Russians* and *Swedes* entered into an agreement, not to suffer Great Britain to export ANY NAVAL STORES from their dominions but in *Russian* or *Swedish* ships, and at their own prices. *Great Britain* was distressed. *Pitch* and *tar* rose to *Three Pounds* a barrel. At length she thought of getting these articles from the colonies; and the attempt succeeding, they fell down to *Fifteen Shillings.* In the year 1756, *Great Britain* was threatened with an invasion. An easterly wind blowing for six

be courageously and constantly opposed. To suffer our ideas to be confounded by *names* on such occasions, would certainly be an *inexcusable weakness,* and probably an *irremediable error.*

We have reason to believe, that several of his Majesty's present ministers are good men, and friends to our country; and it seems not unlikely, that by a particular concurrence of events, we have been treated a little more severely than they wished we should be. *They* might not think it prudent to stem a torrent. But what is the difference to *us,* whether arbitrary acts take their rise from ministers, or are permitted by them? Ought any point to be allowed to a good minister, that should be denied to a bad one?* The mortality of ministers, is a very frail mortality. A —— may succeed a *Shelburne*—A —— may succeed a *Conway.*

We find a new kind of minister lately spoken of at home—"THE MINISTER OF THE HOUSE OF COMMONS." The term seems to have peculiar propriety when referred to these colonies, *with a different meaning annexed to it,* from that in which it is taken there. By the word "minister" we may understand not only a *servant of the crown,* but a *man of influence* among the commons, who regard themselves as having a share in the *sovereignty* over us. The "minister of the house" may, in a point respecting the colonies, be so strong, that the minister of the crown *in* the house, if he is a distinct person, may not choose, even where his sentiments are favorable to us, to come to a pitched battle upon our account. For tho' I have the highest opinion of the deference of the house for the King's minister, yet he may be so good natured, as not to put it to the test, except it be for the mere and immediate profit of his master or himself.

---

weeks, she could not MAN her fleet, and the whole nation was thrown into the utmost consternation. The wind changed. The *American* ships arrived. The fleet sailed in ten or fifteen days. There are some other reflections on this subject, worthy of the most deliberate attention of the *British* parliament; but they are of such a nature, that I do not choose to mention them publicly. I thought it my duty, in the year 1765, while the *Stamp Act* was in suspense, to write my sentiments to a gentleman of great influence at home, who afterwards distinguished himself, by espousing our cause, in the debates concerning the repeal of that act.

* *Ubi imperium ad ignaros aut minus bonos pervenit; novum illud exemplum, ab dignis & idoneis, ad indignos & non idoneos transfeltur.* (*Sall.* Bell. Cat § 50)

But whatever kind of *minister* he is, that attempts to innovate a *single* iota in the privileges of these colonies, him I hope you will *undauntedly oppose;* and that you will never suffer yourselves to be either *cheated* or *frightened* into any *unworthy obsequiousness.* On such emergencies you may surely, without presumption, believe, that ALMIGHTY GOD himself will look down upon your righteous contest with gracious approbation. You will be a "*band of brothers,*" cemented by the dearest ties—and strengthened with inconceivable supplies of force and constancy, by that sympathetic ardor, which animates good men, confederated in a good cause. Your *honor* and *welfare* will be, as they now are, most intimately concerned; and besides—*you are assigned by divine providence,* in the appointed order of things, the *protectors of unborn ages,* whose *fate* depends upon your *virtue.* Whether *they* shall arise the *generous* and *indisputable heirs* of the noblest patrimonies, or the *dastardly and hereditary drudges* of imperious task-masters, YOU MUST DETERMINE.

To discharge this double duty to *yourselves,* and to your *posterity,* you have nothing to do, but to call forth into use the *good sense* and *spirit* of which you are possessed. You have nothing to do, but to conduct your affairs *peaceably—prudently—firmly—jointly.* By *these means* you will support the character of *freemen,* without losing that of *faithful subjects*—a good character in any government—one of the best under a *British* government. You will *prove,* that *Americans* have that true *magnanimity* of soul, that can resent injuries, without falling into rage; and that tho' your devotion to *Great Britain* is the most affectionate, yet you can make PROPER DISTINCTIONS, and know what you owe *to yourselves,* as well as *to her*—You will, at the same time that you advance your *interests,* advance your *reputation*—You will convince the world of the *justice of your demands,* and the *purity of your intentions.* While all mankind must, with unceasing applauses, confess, that YOU indeed DESERVE liberty, who so *well understand* it, so *passionately love* it, so *temperately enjoy* it, and so *wisely, bravely,* and *virtuously assert, maintain,* and *defend* it.

"Certe ego libertatem, quae mihi a parente meo tradita est, experiar: Verum id frustra an ob rem faciam, in vestra manu situm est, quirites."

> For my part, I am resolved to contend for the liberty delivered down to me by my ancestors, but whether I shall do it effectually or not, depends on you, my countrymen. "How littlesoever one is able to write, yet when the liberties of one's country are threatened, it is still more difficult to be silent."

A Farmer

Is there not the strongest probability, that if the universal sense of these colonies is immediately expressed by RESOLVES of the assemblies, in support of their rights, by INSTRUCTIONS to their agents on the subject, and by PETITIONS to the crown and parliament for redress, these measures will have the same success now, that they had in the time of the *STAMP ACT.*

Observations Leading to a Fair Examination of the System of Government Proposed by the Late Convention; and to Several Essential and Necessary Alterations in it. In a Number of

Letters from the Federal Farmer to the Republican

Richard Henry Lee

LETTER I

October 8, 1787.

Dear Sir,

My letters to you last winter, on the subject of a well-balanced national government for the United States, were the result of free enquiry; when I passed from that subject to enquiries relative to our commerce, revenues, past administration, etc. I anticipated the anxieties I feel, on carefully examining the plan of government proposed by the convention. It appears to be a plan retaining some federal features; but to be the first important step, and to aim strongly to one consolidated government of the United States. It leaves the powers of government, and the representation of the people, so unnaturally divided between the general and state governments, that the operations of our system must be very uncertain. My uniform federal attachments, and the interest I have in the protection of property, and a steady execution of the laws, will convince you, that, if I am under any bias at all, it is in favor of any general system which shall promise those advantages. The instability of our laws increases my wishes for firm and steady government; but then, I can consent to no government, which, in my opinion, is not calculated equally to preserve the rights of all orders of men in the community. My object has been to join with those who have endeavored to supply the defects in the forms of our governments by a steady and proper administration of them. Though I have long apprehended that fraudulent debtors, and embarrassed men, on the one hand, and men, on the other, unfriendly to republican equality, would produce an uneasiness among the people, and prepare the way, not for cool and deliberate reforms in the governments, but for changes calculated to promote the interests of particular orders of men. Acquit me, sir, of any agency in the formation of the new system; I shall be satisfied with seeing, if it shall be adopted, a prudent administration. Indeed I am so much convinced of the truth of Pope's maxim, that "That which is best administered is best," that I am much inclined to subscribe to it from experience. I am not disposed to unreasonably contend about forms. I know our situation is critical, and it behooves us to make the best of it. A federal government of some sort is necessary. We have suffered the present to languish; and whether the confederation was capable or not originally of answering any valuable purposes, it is now but of little importance. I will pass by the men, and states, who have been particularly instrumental in preparing the way for a change, and, perhaps, for governments not very favorable to the people at large. A constitution is now presented, which we may reject, or which we may accept, with or without amendments; and to which point we ought to direct our exertions is the question. To determine this question, with propriety, we must attentively examine the system itself, and the probable consequences of either step. This I shall endeavor to do, so far as I am able, with candor and fairness; and leave you to decide upon the propriety of my opinions, the weight of my reasons, and how far my conclusions are well drawn. Whatever may be the conduct of others, on the present occasion, I do not mean, hastily and positively to decide on the merits of the constitution proposed. I shall be open to conviction and always disposed to adopt that which, all things considered, shall appear to me to be most for the happiness of the community. It must be granted, that if men hastily and blindly adopt a system of government, they will as hastily and as blindly be led to alter or abolish it; and changes must ensue, one after another, till the peaceable and better part of the community will grow weary with changes, tumults and disorders, and be disposed to accept any government, however despotic, that shall promise stability and firmness.

The first principal question that occurs, is, Whether, considering our situation, we ought to precipitate the adoption of the proposed constitution? If we remain cool and temperate, we are in no immediate danger of any commotions; we are in a state of perfect peace, and in no danger of invasions; the state governments are in the full exercise of their powers; and our governments answer all present exigencies, except the regulation of trade, securing credit, in some cases, and providing for the interest, in some instances, of the public debts; and whether we adopt a change three or nine months hence, can make but little odds with the private circumstances of individuals; their happiness and prosperity, after all, depend principally upon their own exertions. We are hardly recovered from a long and distressing war: The farmers, fishermen, etc. have not yet fully repaired the waste made by it. Industry and frugality are again assuming their proper station. Private debts are lessened, and public debts incurred by the war have been, by various ways, diminished; and the public lands have now become a productive source for diminishing them much more. I know uneasy men, who wish very much to precipitate, do not admit all these facts; but they are facts well known to all men who are thoroughly informed in the affairs of this country. It must, however, be admitted, that our federal system is defective, and that some of the state governments are not well administered; but, then, we impute to the defects in our governments many evils and embarrassments which are most clearly the result of the late war. We must allow men to conduct on the present occasion, as on all similar ones. They will urge a thousand pretenses to answer their purposes on both sides. When we want a man to change his condition, we describe it as miserable, wretched, and despised; and draw a pleading picture of that which we would have him assume. And when we wish the contrary, we reverse our descriptions. Whenever a clamor is raised, and idle men get to work, it is highly necessary to examine facts carefully, and without unreasonably suspecting men of falsehood, to examine and inquire attentively, under what impressions they act. It is too often the case in political concerns, that men state facts not as they are, but as they wish them to be; and almost every man, by calling to mind past scenes, will find this to be true.

Nothing by the passions of ambitious, impatient, or disorderly men, I conceive, will plunge us into commotions, if time should be taken fully to examine and consider the system proposed. Men who feel easy in their circumstances, and such as are not sanguine in their expectations relative to the consequences of the proposed change, will remain quiet under the existing governments. Many commercial and monied men, who are uneasy, not without just cause, ought to be respected; and, by no means, unreasonably disappointed in their expectations and hopes; but as to those who expect employments under the new constitution; as to those weak and ardent men who always expect to be gainers by revolutions and whose lot it generally is to get out of one difficulty into another, they are very little to be regarded: and as to those who designedly avail themselves of this weakness and ardor, they are to be despised. It is natural for men, who wish to hasten the adoption of a measure, to tell us, now is the crisis—now is the critical moment which must be seized, or all will be lost: and to shut the door against free enquiry, whenever conscious the thing presented has defects in it, which time and investigation will probably discover. This has been the custom of tyrants and their dependents in all ages. If it is true, what has been so often said, that the people of this country cannot change their condition for the worse, I presume it still behooves them to endeavor deliberately to change it for the better. The fickle and ardent, in any community, are the proper tools for establishing despotic government. But it is deliberate and thinking men, who must establish and secure governments on free principles. Before they decide on the plan proposed, they will inquire whether it will probably be a blessing or a curse to this people.

The present moment discovers a new face in our affairs. Our object has been all along, to reform our federal system, and to strengthen our governments—to establish peace, order and justice in the community—but a new object now presents. The plan of government now proposed is evidently calculated totally to change, in time, our condition as a people. Instead of being thirteen republics, under a federal head, it is clearly designed to make us one consolidated government. Of this, I think, I shall fully convince you, in my following letters on this subject. This consolidation of the states has been the object of several men in this country for some time past. Whether such a change can ever be effected in any manner; whether it can be effected without convulsions and civil wars; whether such a change will not totally destroy the liberties of this country—time only can determine.

To have a just idea of the government before us, and to show that a consolidated one is the object in view, it is necessary not only to examine the plan, but also its history, and the politics of its particular friends.

The confederation was formed when great confidence was placed in the voluntary exertions of individuals, and of the respective states; and the framers of it, to guard against usurpation, so limited and checked the powers, that, in many respects, they are inadequate to the exigencies of the union. We find, therefore, members of congress urging alterations in the federal system almost as soon as it was adopted. It was early proposed to vest congress with powers to levy an impost, to regulate trade, etc. but such was known to be the caution of the states in parting with power, that the vestment, even of these, was proposed to be under several checks and limitations. During the war, the general confusion, and the introduction of paper money, infused in the minds of people vague ideas respecting government and credit. We expected too much from the return of peace, and of course we have been disappointed. Our governments have been new and unsettled; and several legislatures, by making tender, suspension, and paper money laws, have given just cause of uneasiness to creditors. By these and other causes, several orders of men in the community have been prepared, by degrees, for a change of government; and this very abuse of power in the legislatures, which, in some cases, has been charged upon the democratic part of the community, has furnished aristocratical men with those very weapons, and those very means, with which, in great measure, they are rapidly effecting their favorite object. And should an oppressive government be the consequence of the proposed change, posterity may reproach not only a few overbearing unprincipled men, but those parties in the states which have misused their powers.

The conduct of several legislatures, touching paper money, and tender laws, has prepared many honest men for changes in government, which otherwise they would not have thought of—when by the evils, on the one hand, and by the secret instigations of artful men, on the other, the minds of men were become sufficiently uneasy, a bold step was taken, which is usually followed by a revolution, or a civil war. A general convention for mere commercial purposes was moved for—the authors of this measure saw that the people's attention was turned solely to the amendment of the federal system; and that, had the idea of a total change been started, probably no state would have appointed members to the convention. The idea of destroying, ultimately, the state government, and forming one consolidated system, could not have been admitted—a convention, therefore, merely for vesting in congress power to regulate trade was proposed. This was pleasing to the commercial towns; and the landed people had little or no concern about it. September, 1786, a few men from the middle states met at Annapolis, and hastily proposed a convention to be held in May, 1787, for the purpose, generally, of amending the confederation—this was done before the delegates of Massachusetts, and of the other states arrived—still not a word was said about destroying the old constitution, and making a new one—The states still unsuspecting, and not aware that they were passing the Rubicon, appointed members to the new convention, for the sole and express purpose of revising and amending the confederation—and, probably, not one man in ten thousand in the United States, till within these ten or twelve days, had an idea that the old ship was to be destroyed, and he put to the alternative of embarking in the new ship presented, or of being left in danger of sinking—The states, I believe, universally supposed the convention would report alterations in the confederation, which would pass an examination in congress, and after being agreed to there, would be confirmed by all the legislatures, or be rejected. Virginia made a very respectable appointment, and placed at the head of it the first man in America: In this appointment there was a mixture of political characters; but Pennsylvania appointed principally those men who are esteemed aristocratical. Here the favorite moment for changing the government was evidently discerned by a few men, who seized it with address. Ten other states appointed, and tho' they chose men principally connected with commerce and the judicial department yet they appointed many good republican characters—had they all attended we should now see, I am persuaded, a better system presented. The non-attendance of eight or nine men, who were appointed members of the convention, I shall ever consider as a very unfortunate event to the United States—Had they attended

I am pretty clear that the result of the convention would not have had that strong tendency to aristocracy now discernable in every part of the plan. There would not have been so great an accumulation of powers, especially as to the internal police of the country, in a few hands, as the constitution reported proposes to vest in them—the young visionary men, and the consolidating aristocracy, would have been more restrained than they have been. Eleven states met in the convention, and after four months close attention presented the new constitution, to be adopted or rejected by the people. The uneasy and fickle part of the community may be prepared to receive any form of government; but, I presume, the enlightened and substantial part will give any constitution presented for their adoption a candid and thorough examination; and silence those designing or empty men, who weakly and rashly attempt to precipitate the adoption of a system of so much importance—We shall view the convention with proper respect—and, at the same time, that we reflect there were men of abilities and integrity in it, we must recollect how disproportionably the democratic and aristocratic parts of the community were represented. Perhaps the judicious friends and opposers of the new constitution will agree, that it is best to let it rest solely on its own merits, or be condemned for its own defects.

In the first place, I shall premise, that the plan proposed is a plan of accommodation—and that it is in this way only, and by giving up a part of our opinions, that we can ever expect to obtain a government founded in freedom and compact. This circumstance candid men will always keep in view, in the discussion of this subject.

The plan proposed appears to be partly federal, but principally, however, calculated ultimately to make the states one consolidated government.

The first interesting question, therefore suggested, is, how far the states can be consolidated into one entire government on free principles. In considering this question extensive objects are to be taken into view, and important changes in the forms of government to be carefully attended to in all their consequences. The happiness of the people at large must be the great object with every honest statesman, and he will direct every movement to this point. If we are so situated as a people, as not to be able to enjoy equal happiness and advantages under one government, the consolidation of the states cannot be admitted.

There are three different forms of free government under which the United States may exist as one nation; and now is, perhaps, the time to determine to which we will direct our views. 1. Distinct republics connected under a federal head. In this case the respective state governments must be the principal guardians of the people's rights, and exclusively regulate their internal police: in them must rest the balance of government. The congress of the states, or federal head, must consist of delegates amenable to, and removable by the respective states: This congress must have general directing powers; powers to require men and monies of the states; to make treaties, peace and war; to direct the operations of armies, etc. Under this federal modification of government, the powers of congress would be rather advisory or recommendatory than coercive. 2. We may do away with the several state governments, and form or consolidate all the states into one entire government, with one executive, one judiciary, and one legislature, consisting of senators and representatives collected from all parts of the union: In this case there would be a complete consolidation of the states. 3. We may consolidate the states as to certain national objects, and leave them severally distinct independent republics, as to internal police generally. Let the general government consist of an executive, a judiciary and balanced legislature, and its powers extend exclusively to all foreign concerns, causes arising on the seas to commerce, imports, armies, navies, Indian affairs, peace and war, and to a few internal concerns of the community; to the coin, post offices, weights and measures, a general plan for the militia, to naturalization, *and, perhaps to bankruptcies*, leaving the internal police of the community, in other respects, exclusively to the state governments; as the administration of justice in all causes arising internally, the laying and collecting of internal taxes, and the forming of the militia according to a general plan prescribed. In this case there would be a complete consolidation, *quoad* certain objects only.

Touching the first, or federal plan, I do not think much can be said in its favor: The sovereignty of the nation, without coercive and efficient powers to collect the strength of it, cannot always be depended on to answer the purposes of government, and in a congress of representatives of sovereign states, there must necessarily be an unreasonable mixture of powers in the same hands.

As to the second, or complete consolidating plan, it deserves to be carefully considered at this time, by every American: If it be impracticable, it is a fatal error to model our governments directing our views ultimately to it.

The third plan, or partial consolidation, is, in my opinion, the only one that can secure the freedom and happiness of this people. I once had some general ideas that the second plan was practicable, but from long attention, and the proceedings of the convention, I am fully satisfied, that this third plan is the only one we can with safety and propriety proceed upon. Making this the standard to point out, with candor and fairness, the parts of the new constitution which appear to be improper, is my object. The convention appears to have proposed the partial consolidation evidently with a view to collect all powers ultimately, in the United States into one entire government; and from its views in this respect, and from the tenacity of the small states to have an equal vote in the senate, probably originated the greatest defects in the proposed plan.

Independent of the opinions of many great authors, that a free elective government cannot be extended over large territories, a few reflections must evince, that one government and general legislation alone, never can extend equal benefits to all parts of the United States: Different laws, customs, and opinions exist in the different states, which by a uniform system of laws would be unreasonably invaded. The United States contain about a million of square miles, and in half a century will, probably, contain ten millions of people; and from the center to the extremes is about 800 miles.

Before we do away the state governments, or adopt measures that will tend to abolish them, and to consolidate the states into one entire government, several principles should be considered and facts ascertained: These, and my examination into the essential parts of the proposed plan, I shall pursue in my next.

Yours Etc.

The Federal Farmer

LETTER II

October 9, 1787.

Dear Sir,

The essential parts of a free and good government are a full and equal representation of the people in the legislature, and the jury trial of the vicinage in the administration of justice—a full and equal representation, is that which possesses the same interests, feelings, opinions, and views the people themselves would were they all assembled—a fair representation, therefore, should be so regulated that every order of men in the community, according to the common course of elections, can have a share in it—in order to allow professional men, merchants, traders, farmers, mechanics, etc. to bring a just proportion of their best informed men respectively into the legislature, the representation must be considerably numerous—We have about 200 state senators in the United States, and a less number than that of federal representatives cannot, clearly, be a full representation of this people, in the affairs of internal taxation and police, were there but one legislature for the whole union. The representation cannot be equal, or the situation of the people proper for one government only—if the extreme parts of the society cannot be represented as fully as the central—It is apparently impracticable that this should be the case in this extensive country—it would be impossible to collect a representation of the parts of the country five, six, and seven hundred miles from the seat of government.

Under one general government alone, there could be but one judiciary, one supreme and a proper number of inferior courts. I think it would be totally impracticable in this case to preserve a due administration of justice, and the real benefits of the jury trial of the vicinage—there are now supreme courts in each state in the union and a great number of county and other courts subordinate to each supreme court—most of these supreme and inferior courts are itinerant, and hold their sessions in different parts every year of their respective states, counties and districts—with all these moving courts, our citizens, from the vast extent of the country must travel very considerable distances from home to find the place where justice is administered. I am not for bringing justice so near to individuals as to afford them any temptation to engage in law suits; though I think it one of the greatest benefits in a good government, that each citizen should find a court of justice within a reasonable distance, perhaps within a day's travel of his home; so that, without great inconveniences and enormous expenses, he may have the advantages of his witnesses and jury—it would be impracticable to derive these advantages from one judiciary—the one supreme court at most could only set in the center of the union, and move once a year into the center of the eastern and southern extremes of it—and, in this case, each citizen, on an average, would travel 150 or 200 miles to find this court—that, however, inferior courts might be properly placed in the different counties, and districts of the union, the appellate jurisdiction would be intolerable and expensive.

If it were possible to consolidate the states, and preserve the features of a free government, still it is evident that the middle states, the parts of the union, about the seat of government, would enjoy great advantages, while the remote states would experience the many inconveniences of remote provinces. Wealth, offices, and the benefits of government would collect in the center: and the extreme states, and their principal towns, become much less important.

There are other considerations which tend to prove that the idea of one consolidated whole, on free principles, is ill-founded—the laws of a free government rest on the confidence of the people and operate gently—and never can extend their influence very far—if they are executed on free principles, about the center, where the benefits of the government induce the people to support it voluntarily; yet they must be executed on the principles of fear and force in the extremes—This has been the case with every extensive republic of which we have any accurate account.

There are certain inalienable and fundamental rights, which in forming the social compact, ought to be explicitly ascertained and fixed—a free and enlightened people, in forming this compact, will not resign all their rights to those who govern, and they will fix limits to their legislators and rulers, which will soon be plainly seen by those who are governed, as well as by those who govern: and the latter will know they cannot be passed unperceived by the former, and without giving a general alarm—These rights should be made the basis of every constitution; and if a people be so situated, or have such different opinions that they cannot agree in ascertaining and fixing them, it is a very strong argument against their attempting to form one entire society, to live under one system of laws only. I confess, I never thought the people of these states differed essentially in these respects; they having derived all these rights from one common source, the British systems; and having in the formation of their state constitutions, discovered that their ideas relative to these rights are very similar. However, it is now said that the states differ so essentially in these respects, and even in the important article of the trial by jury, that when assembled in convention, they can agree to no words by which to establish that trial, or by which to ascertain and establish many other of these rights, as fundamental articles in the social compact. If so, we proceed to consolidate the states on no solid basis whatever.

But I do not pay much regard to the reasons given for not bottoming the new constitution on a better bill of rights. I still believe a complete federal bill of rights to be very practicable. Nevertheless I acknowledge the proceedings of the convention furnish my mind with many new and strong reasons, against a complete consolidation of the states. They tend to convince me, that it cannot be carried with propriety very far—that the convention have gone much farther in one respect than they found it practicable to go in another; that is, they propose to lodge in the general government very extensive powers—*powers* nearly, if not altogether, complete and unlimited, over the purse and the sword. But, in its organization, they furnish the strongest proof that the proper limbs, or parts of a government, to support and execute those powers on proper principles (or in which they can be safely lodged) cannot be formed. These powers must be lodged somewhere in every society; but then they should be lodged where the strength and guardians of the people are collected. They can be wielded, or safely used, in a free country only by an able executive and judiciary, a respectable senate, and a secure, full, and equal representation of the people. I think the principles I have premised or brought into view, are well founded—I think they will not be denied by any fair reasoner. It is in connection with these, and other solid principles, we are to examine the constitution. It is not a few democratic phrases, or a few well formed features, that will prove its merits; or a few small omissions that will produce its rejection among men of sense; they will inquire what are the essential powers in a community, and what are nominal ones; where and how the essential powers shall be lodged to secure government, and to secure true liberty.

In examining the proposed constitution carefully, we must clearly perceive an unnatural separation of these powers from the substantial representation of the people. The state governments will exist, with all their governors, senators, representatives, officers and expenses; in these will be nineteen-twentieths of the representatives of the people; they will have a near connection, and their members an immediate intercourse with the people; and the probability is, that the state governments will possess the confidence of the people, and be considered generally as their immediate guardians.

The general government will consist of a new species of executive, a small senate, and a very small house of representatives. As many citizens will be more than three hundred miles from the seat of this government as will be nearer to it, its judges and officers cannot be very numerous, without making our governments very expensive. Thus will stand the state and the general governments, should the constitution be adopted without any alterations in their organization; but as to powers, the general government will possess all essential ones, at least on paper, and those of the states a mere shadow of power. And therefore, unless the people shall make some great exertions to restore to the state governments their powers in matters of internal police; as the powers to lay and collect, exclusively, internal taxes, to govern the militia, and to hold the decisions of their own judicial courts upon their own laws final, the balance cannot possibly continue long; but the state governments must be annihilated, or continue to exist for no purpose.

It is however to be observed, that many of the essential powers given the national government are not exclusively given; and the general government may have prudence enough to forbear the exercise of those which may still be exercised by the respective states. But this cannot justify the impropriety of giving powers, the exercise of which prudent men will not attempt, and imprudent men will, or probably can, exercise only in a manner destructive of free government. The general government, organized as it is, may be adequate to many valuable objects, and be able to carry its laws into execution on proper principles in several cases; but I think its warmest friends will not contend, that it can carry all the powers proposed to be lodged in it into effect, without calling to its aid a military force, which must very soon destroy all elective governments in the country, produce anarchy or establish despotism. Though we cannot have now a complete idea of what will be the operations of the proposed system, we may, allowing things to have their common course, have a very tolerable one. The powers lodged in the general government, if exercised by it, must intimately affect the internal police of the states, as well as external concerns; and there is no reason to expect the numerous state governments, and their connections, will be very friendly to the execution of federal laws in those internal affairs which hitherto have been under their own immediate management. There is more reason to believe, that the general government, far removed from the people, and none of its members elected oftener than once in two years, will be forgot or neglected, and its laws in many cases disregarded, unless a multitude of officers and military force be continually kept in view, and employed to enforce the execution of the laws, and to make the government feared and respected. No position can be truer than this. That in this country either neglected laws, or a military execution of them, must lead to a revolution, and to the destruction of freedom. Neglected laws must first lead to anarchy and confusion; and a military execution of laws is only a shorter way to the same point—despotic government.

Yours Etc.

The Federal Farmer

LETTER III

October 10, 1787.

Dear Sir,

The great object of a free people must be so to form their government and laws and so to administer them, as to create a confidence in, and respect for the laws; and thereby induce the sensible and virtuous part of the community to declare in favor of the laws, and to support them without an expensive military force. I wish, though I confess I have not much hope, that this may be the case with the laws of congress under the new constitution. I am fully convinced that we must organize the national government on different principles, and make the parts of it more efficient, and secure in it more effectually the different interests in the community; or else leave in the state governments some powers proposed to be lodged in it—at least till such an organization shall be found to be practicable. Not sanguine in my expectations of a good federal administration, and satisfied, as I am, of the impracticability of consolidating the states, and at the same time of preserving the rights of the people at large, I believe we ought still to leave some of these powers in the state governments, in which the people, in fact, will still be represented—to define some other powers proposed to be vested in the general government, more carefully, and to establish a few principles to secure a proper exercise of the powers given it. It is not my object to multiply objections, or to contend about inconsiderable powers or amendments; I wish the system adopted with a few alterations; but those, in my mind, are essential ones; if adopted without, every good citizen will acquiesce, though I shall consider the duration of our governments, and the liberties of this people, very much dependent on the administration of the general government. A wise and honest administration, may make the people happy under any government; but necessity only can justify even our leaving open avenues to the abuse of power, by wicked, unthinking, or ambitious men. I will examine, first, the organization of the proposed government, in order to judge; 2nd, with propriety, what powers are improperly, at least prematurely lodged in it. I shall examine, 3rd, the undefined powers; and 4th, those powers, the exercise of which is not secured on safe and proper ground.

First. As to the organization—the house of representatives, the democrative branch, as it is called, is to consist of 65 members: that is, about one representative for fifty thousand inhabitants, to be chosen biennially—the federal legislature may increase this number to one for each thirty thousand inhabitants, abating fractional numbers in each state. Thirty-three representatives will make a quorum for doing business, and a majority of those present determine the sense of the house. I have no idea that the interests, feelings, and opinions of three or four millions of people, especially touching internal taxation, can be collected in such a house. In the nature of things, nine times in ten, men of the elevated classes in the community only can be chosen—Connecticut, for instance, will have five representatives—

not one man in a hundred of those who form the democrative branch in the state legislature, will, on a fair computation, be one of the five—The people of this country, in one sense, may all be democratic; but if we make the proper distinction between the few men of wealth and abilities, and consider them, as we ought, as the natural aristocracy of the country, and the great body of the people, the middle and lower classes, as the democracy, this federal representative branch will have but very little democracy in it, even this small representation is not secured on proper principles. The branches of the legislature are essential parts of the fundamental compact and ought to be so fixed by the people, that the legislature cannot alter itself by modifying the elections of its own members. This, by a part of art. 1. sect. 4. the general legislature may do. It may evidently so regulate elections as to secure the choice of any particular description of men. It may make the whole state one district—make the capital, or any place in the state, the place or places of election—it may declare that the five men (or whatever the number may be the state may choose) who shall have the most votes shall be considered as chosen—In this case it is easy to perceive how the people who live scattered in the inland towns will bestow their votes on different men—and how a few men in a city, in any order or profession, may unite and place any five men they please highest among those that may be voted for—and all this may be done constitutionally, and by those silent operations, which are not immediately perceived by the people in general. I know it is urged, that the general legislature will be disposed to regulate elections on fair and just principles: This may be true—good men will generally govern well with almost any constitution: but why in laying the foundation of the social system, need we unnecessarily leave a door open to improper regulations? This is a very general and unguarded clause, and many evils may flow from that part which authorizes the congress to regulate elections—Were it omitted, the regulations of elections would be solely in the respective states, where the people are substantially represented; and where the elections ought to be regulated, otherwise to secure a representation from all parts of the community, in making the constitution, we ought to provide for dividing each state into a proper number of districts, and for confining the electors in each district to the choice of some men, who shall have a permanent interest and residence in it; and also for this essential object, that the representative elected shall have a majority of the votes of those electors who shall attend and give their votes.

In considering the practicability of having a full and equal representation of the people from all parts of the union, not only distances and different opinions, customs, and views, common in extensive tracts of country, are to be taken into view, but many differences peculiar to eastern, middle and southern states. These differences are not so perceivable among the members of congress, and men of general information in the states, as among the men who would properly form the democratic branch. The eastern states are very democratic, and composed chiefly of moderate freeholders: they have but few rich men and no slaves; the southern states are composed chiefly of rich planters and slaves; they have but few moderate freeholders, and the prevailing influence, in them, is generally a dissipated aristocracy. The middle states partake partly of the eastern, and partly of the southern character.

Perhaps, nothing could be more disjointed, unwieldy and incompetent to doing business with harmony and dispatch, than a federal house of representatives properly numerous for the great objects of taxation, etc. collected from the several states; whether such men would ever act in concert; whether they would not worry along a few years, and then be the means of separating the parts of the union, is very problematical—View this system in whatever form we can, propriety brings us still to this point, a federal government possessed of general and complete powers, as to those national objects which cannot well come under the cognizance of the internal laws of the respective states, and this federal government, accordingly, consisting of branches not very numerous.

The house of representatives is on the plan of consolidation, but the senate is entirely on the federal plan; and Delaware will have as much constitutional influence in the senate, as the largest state in the union: and in this senate are lodged legislative, executive and judicial powers: Ten states in this union urge that they are small states, nine of which were present in the convention. They were interested in collecting large powers into the hands of the senate, in which each state still will have its equal share of power. I suppose it was impracticable for the three large states, as they were called, to get the senate formed on any other principles: But this only proves, that we cannot form one general government on equal and just principles—and proves, that we ought not to lodge in it such extensive powers before we are convinced of the practicability of organizing it on just and equal principles. The senate will consist of two members from each state, chosen by the state legislatures, every sixth year. The clause referred to, respecting the elections of representatives, empowers the general legislature to regulate the elections of senators also, "except as to the places of choosing senators." There is, therefore, but little more security in the elections than in those of representatives: Fourteen senators make a quorum for business, and a majority of the senators present give the vote of the senate, except in giving judgment upon an impeachment, or in making treaties, or in expelling a member, when two-thirds of the senators present must agree—The members of the legislature are not excluded from being elected to any military offices, or any civil offices, except those created, or the emoluments of which shall be increased by themselves: two-thirds of the members present, of either house, may expel a member at pleasure. The senate is an independent branch of the legislature, a court for trying impeachments, and also a part of the executive, having a negative in the making of all treaties, and in appointing almost all officers.

The vice-president is not a very important, if not an unnecessary part of the system—he may be a part of the senate at one period, and act as the supreme executive magistrate at another—The election of this officer, as well as of the president of the United States, seems to be properly secured; but when we examine the powers of the president, and the forms of the executive, we shall perceive that the general government, in this part, will have a strong tendency to aristocracy, or the government of the few. The executive is, in fact, the president and senate in all transactions of any importance; the president is connected with, or tied to the senate; he may always act with the senate, but never can effectually counteract its views: The president can appoint no officer, civil or military, who shall not be agreeable to the senate; and the presumption is, that the will of so important a body will not be very easily controlled, and that it will exercise its powers with great address.

In the judicial department, powers ever kept distinct in well-balanced governments, are not less improperly blended in the hands of the same men—in the judges of the supreme court is lodged, the law, the equity and the fact. It is not necessary to pursue the minute organical parts of the general government proposed. There were various interests in the convention to be reconciled, especially of large and small states; of carrying and non-carrying states; and of states more and states less democratic—vast labor and attention were by the convention bestowed on the organization of the parts of the constitution offered; still it is acknowledged there are many things radically wrong in the essential parts of this constitution—but it is said that these are the result of our situation: On a full examination of the subject, I believe it; but what do the laborious inquiries and determinations of the convention prove? If they prove anything, they prove that we cannot consolidate the states on proper principles: The organization of the government presented proves, that we cannot form a general government in which all power can be safely lodged; and a little attention to the parts of the one proposed will make it appear very evident, that all the powers proposed to be lodged in it, will not be then well deposited, either for the purposes of government, or the preservation of liberty. I will suppose no abuse of powers in those cases, in which the abuse of it is not well guarded against—I will suppose the words authorizing the general government to regulate the elections of its own members struck out of the plan, or free district elections, in each state, amply secured—That the small representation provided for shall be as fair and equal as it is capable of being made—I will suppose the judicial department regulated on pure principles, by future laws, as far as it can be by the constitution, and consistent with the situation of the country—still there will be an unreasonable accumulation of powers in the general government, if all be granted, enumerated in the plan proposed. The plan does not present a well-balanced government. The senatorial branch of the legislative and the executive are substantially united, and the president, or the first executive magistrate, may aid the senatorial interest when weakest, but never can effectually support the democratic, however it may be oppressed—the excellency, in my mind, of a well-balanced government is that it consists of distinct branches, each sufficiently strong and independent to keep its own station, and to aid either of the other branches which may occasionally want aid.

The convention found that any but a small house of representatives would be expensive, and that it would be impracticable to assemble a large number of representatives. Not only the determination of the convention in this case, but the situation of the states, proves the impracticability of collecting, in any one point, a proper representation.

The formation of the senate, and the smallness of the house, being, therefore, the result of our situation, and the actual state of things, the evils which may attend the exercise of many powers in this national government may be considered as without a remedy.

All officers are impeachable before the senate only—before the men by whom they are appointed, or who are consenting to the appointment of these officers. No judgment of conviction, on an impeachment, can be given unless two-thirds of the senators agree. Under these circumstances the right of impeachment, in the house, can be of but little importance; the house cannot expect often to convict the offender; and, therefore, probably, will but seldom or never exercise the right. In addition to the insecurity and inconveniences attending this organization beforementioned, it may be observed, that it is extremely difficult to secure the people against the fatal effects of corruption and influence. The power of making any law will be in the president, eight senators, and seventeen representatives, relative to the important objects enumerated in the constitution. Where there is a small representation a sufficient number to carry any measure, may, with ease, be influenced by bribes, offices and civilities; they may easily form private juntas, and outdoor meetings, agree on measures, and carry them by silent votes.

Impressed, as I am, with a sense of the difficulties there are in the way of forming the parts of a federal government on proper principles, and seeing a government so unsubstantially organized, after so arduous an attempt has been made, I am led to believe, that powers ought to be given to it with great care and caution.

In the second place it is necessary, therefore, to examine the extent, and the probable operations of some of those extensive powers proposed to be vested in this government. These powers, legislative, executive, and judicial, respect internal as well as external objects. Those respecting external objects, as all foreign concerns, commerce, imposts, all causes arising on the seas, peace and war, and Indian affairs, can be lodged nowhere else, with any propriety, but in this government. Many powers that respect internal objects ought clearly to be lodged in it; as those to regulate trade between the states, weights and measures, the coin or current monies, post offices, naturalization, etc. These powers may be exercised without essentially affecting the internal police of the respective states: But powers to levy and collect internal taxes, to form the militia, to make bankrupt laws, and to decide on appeals, questions arising on the internal laws of the respective states, are of a very serious nature, and carry with them almost all other powers. These taken in connection with the others, and powers to raise armies and build navies, proposed to be lodged in this government, appear to me to comprehend all the essential powers in the community, and those which will be left to the states will be of no great importance.

A power to lay and collect taxes at discretion, is, in itself, of very great importance. By means of taxes, the government may command the whole or any part of the subject's property. Taxes may be of various kinds; but there is a strong distinction between external and internal taxes. External taxes are impost duties, which are laid on imported goods; they may usually be collected in a few seaport towns, and of a few individuals, though ultimately paid by the consumer; a few officers can collect them, and they can be carried no higher than trade will bear, or smuggling permit—that in the very nature of commerce, bounds are set to them. But internal taxes, as poll and land taxes, excises, duties on all written instruments, etc. may fix themselves on every person and species of property in the community; they may be carried to any lengths, and in proportion as they are extended, numerous officers must be employed to assess them, and to enforce the collection of them. In the United Netherlands the general government has complete powers as to external taxation; but as to internal taxes, it makes requisitions on the provinces. Internal taxation in this country is more important, as the country is so very extensive. As many assessors and collectors of federal taxes will be above three hundred miles from the seat of the federal government as will be less. Besides, to lay and collect internal taxes, in this extensive country, must require a great number of congressional ordinances, immediately operating upon the body of the people; these must continually interfere with the state laws, and thereby produce disorder and general dissatisfaction, till the one system of laws or the other, operating upon the same subjects, shall be abolished. These ordinances alone, to say nothing of those respecting the militia, coin, commerce, federal judiciary, etc. etc. will probably soon defeat the operations of the state laws and governments.

Should the general government think it politic, as some administrations (if not all) probably will, to look for a support in a system of influence, the government will take every occasion to multiply laws, and officers to execute them, considering these as so many necessary props for its own support. Should this system of policy be adopted, taxes more productive than the impost duties will, probably, be wanted to support the government, and to discharge foreign demands, without leaving anything for the domestic creditors. The internal sources of taxation then must be called into operation, and internal tax laws and federal assessors and collectors spread over this immense country. All these circumstances considered, is it wise, prudent, or safe, to vest the powers of laying and collecting internal taxes in the general government, while imperfectly organized and inadequate; and to trust to amending it hereafter, and making it adequate to this purpose? Is it not only unsafe but absurd to lodge power in a government before it is fitted to receive it? It is confessed that this power and representation ought to go together. Why give the power first? Why give the power to the few, who, when possessed of it, may have address enough to prevent the increase of representation? Why not keep the power, and, when necessary, amend the constitution, and add to its other parts this power, and a proper increase of representation at the same time? Then men who may want the power will be under strong inducements to let in the people, by their representatives, into the government, to hold their due proportion of this power. If a proper representation be impracticable, then we shall see this power resting in the states, where it at present ought to be, and not inconsiderately given up.

When I recollect how lately congress, conventions, legislatures, and people contended in the cause of liberty, and carefully weighed the importance of taxation, I can scarcely believe we are serious in proposing to vest the powers of laying and collecting internal taxes in a government so imperfectly organized for such purposes. Should the United States be taxed by a house of representatives of two hundred members, which would be about fifteen members for Connecticut, twenty-five for Massachusetts, etc., still the middle and lower classes of people could have no great share, in fact, in taxation. I am aware it is said, that the representation proposed by the new constitution is sufficiently numerous; it may be for many purposes; but to suppose that this branch is sufficiently numerous to guard the rights of the people in the administration of the government, in which the purse and sword are placed, seems to argue that we have forgotten what the true meaning of representation is. I am sensible also, that it is said that congress will not attempt to lay and collect internal taxes; that it is necessary for them to have the power, though it cannot probably be exercised. I admit that it is not probable that any prudent congress will attempt to lay and collect internal taxes, especially direct taxes: but this only proves that the power would be improperly lodged in congress, and that it might be abused by imprudent and designing men.

I have heard several gentlemen, to get rid of objections to this part of the constitution, attempt to construe the powers relative to direct taxes, as those who object to it would have them; as to these, it is said, that congress will only have power to make requisitions, leaving it to the states to lay and collect them. I see but very little color for this construction, and the attempt only proves that this part of the plan cannot be defended. By this plan there can be no doubt, but that the powers of congress will be complete as to all kinds of taxes whatever—Further, as to internal taxes, the state governments will have concurrent powers with the general government, and both may tax the same objects in the same year; and the objection that the general government may suspend a state tax, as a necessary measure for the promoting the collection of a federal tax, is not without foundation. As the states owe large debts, and have large demands upon them individually, there clearly would be a propriety in leaving in their possession exclusively, some of the internal sources of taxation, at least until the federal representation shall be properly increased: The power in the general government to lay and collect internal taxes, will render its powers respecting armies, navies and the militia, the more exceptionable. By the constitution it is proposed that congress shall have power "to raise and support armies, but no appropriation of money to that use shall be for a longer term than two years; to provide and maintain a navy; to provide for calling forth the militia to execute the laws of the union; suppress insurrections, and repel invasions; to provide for organizing, arming, and disciplining the militia; reserving to the states the right to appoint the officers, and to train the militia according to the discipline prescribed by congress; congress will have unlimited power to raise armies, and to engage officers and men for any number of years; but a legislative act applying money for their support can have operation for no longer term than two years, and if a subsequent congress do not within the two years renew the appropriation, or further appropriate monies for the use of the army, the army will be left to take care of itself. When an army shall once be raised for a number of years, it is not probable that it will find much difficulty in getting congress to pass laws for applying monies to its support. I see so many men in America fond of a standing army, and especially among those who probably will have a large share in administering the federal system; it is very evident to me, that we shall have a large standing army as soon as the monies to support them can be possibly found. An army is a very agreeable place of employment for the young gentlemen of many families. A power to raise armies must be lodged some where; still this will not justify the lodging this power in a bare majority of so few men without any checks; or in the government in which the great body of the people, in the nature of things, will be only nominally represented. In the state governments the great body of the people, the yeomanry, etc. of the country, are represented: It is true they will choose the members of congress, and may now and then choose a man of their own way of thinking; but it is impossible for forty, or thirty thousand people in this country, one time in ten to find a man who can possess similar feelings, views, and interests with themselves: Powers to lay and collect taxes and to raise armies are of the greatest moment; for carrying them into effect, laws need not be frequently made, and the yeomanry, etc. of the country ought substantially to have a check upon the passing of these laws; this check ought to be placed in the legislatures, or at least, in the few men the common people of the country will, probably, have in congress, in the true sense of the word, "from among themselves." It is true, the yeomanry of the country possess the lands, the weight of property, possess arms, and are too strong a body of men to be openly offended—and, therefore, it is urged, they will take care of themselves, that men who shall govern will not dare pay any disrespect to their opinions. It is easily perceived, that if they have not their proper negative upon passing laws in congress, or on the passage of laws relative to taxes and armies, they may in twenty or thirty years be by means imperceptible to them, totally deprived of that boasted weight and strength: This may be done in a great measure by congress, if disposed to do it, by modelling the militia. Should one fifth, or one eighth part of the men capable of bearing arms, be made a select militia, as has been proposed, and those the young and ardent part of the community, possessed of but little or no property, and all the others put upon a plan that will render them of no importance, the former will answer all the purposes of an army, while the latter will be defenseless. The state must train the militia in such form and according to such systems and rules as congress shall prescribe: and the only actual influence the respective states will have respecting the militia will be in appointing the officers. I see no provision made for calling out the *posse commitatus* for executing the laws of the union, but provision is made for congress to call forth the militia for the execution of them—and the militia in general, or any select part of it, may be called out under military officers, instead of the sheriff to enforce an execution of federal laws, in the first instance and thereby introduce an entirely military execution of the laws. I know that powers to raise taxes, to regulate the military strength of the community on some uniform plan, to provide for its defense and internal order, and for duly executing the laws, must be lodged somewhere; but still we ought not so to lodge them, as evidently to give one order of men in the community, undue advantages over others; or commit the many to the mercy, prudence, and moderation of the few. And so far as it may be necessary to lodge any of the peculiar powers in the general government, a more safe exercise of them ought to be secured, by requiring the consent of two-thirds or three-fourths of congress thereto—until the federal representation can be increased, so that the democratic members in congress may stand some tolerable chance of a reasonable negative, in behalf of the numerous, important, and democratic part of the community.

I am not sufficiently acquainted with the laws and internal police of all the states to discern fully, how general bankrupt laws made by the union, would affect them, or promote the public good. I believe the property of debtors, in the several states, is held responsible for their debts in modes and forms very different. If uniform bankrupt laws can be made without producing real and substantial inconveniences, I wish them to be made by congress.

There are some powers proposed to be lodged in the general government in the judicial department, I think very unnecessarily. I mean powers respecting questions arising upon the internal laws of the respective states. It is proper the federal judiciary should have powers co-extensive with the federal legislature—that is, the power of deciding finally on the laws of the union. By art. 3. sect. 2. the powers of the federal judiciary are extended (among other things) to all cases between a state and citizens of another state—between citizens of different states—between a state or the citizens thereof, and foreign states, citizens or subjects. Actions in all these cases, except against a state government, are now brought and finally determined in the law courts of the states respectively; and as there are no words to exclude these courts of their jurisdiction in these cases, they will have concurrent jurisdiction with the inferior federal courts in them; and, therefore, if the new constitution be adopted without any amendment in this respect, all those numerous actions, now brought in the state courts between our citizens and foreigners, between citizens of different states, by state governments against foreigners, and by state governments against citizens of other states, may also be brought in the federal courts; and an appeal will lay in them from the state courts, or federal inferior courts, to the supreme judicial court of the union. In almost all these cases, either party may have the trial by jury in the state courts; excepting paper money and tender laws, which are wisely guarded against in the proposed constitution, justice may be obtained in these courts on reasonable terms; they must be more competent to proper decisions on the laws of their respective states, than the federal courts can possibly be. I do not, in any point of view, see the need of opening a new jurisdiction to these cases—of opening a new scene of expensive law suits—of suffering foreigners, and citizens of different states, to drag each other many hundred miles into the federal courts. It is true, those courts may be so organized by a wise and prudent legislature, as to make the obtaining of justice in them tolerably easy; they may in general be organized on the common law principles of the country: But this benefit is by no means secured by the constitution. The trial by jury is secured only in those few criminal cases, to which the federal laws will extend—as crimes committed on the seas, against the laws of nations, treason, and counterfeiting the federal securities and coin: But even in these cases, the jury trial of the vicinage is not secured—particularly in the large states, a citizen may be tried for a crime committed in the state, and yet tried in some states 500 miles from the place where it was committed; but the jury trial is not secured at all in civil cases. Though the convention have not established this trial, it is to be hoped that congress, in putting the new system into execution, will do it by a legislative act, in all cases in which it can be done with propriety. Whether the jury trial is not excluded [from] the supreme judicial court, is an important question. By art. 3. sect. 2. all cases affecting ambassadors, other public ministers, and consuls, and in those cases in which a state shall be party, the supreme court shall have jurisdiction. In all the other cases beforementioned, the supreme court shall have appellate jurisdiction, both as to *law and fact*, with such exception, and under such regulations, as the congress shall make. By court is understood a court consisting of judges; and the idea of a jury is excluded. This court, or the judges, are to have jurisdiction on appeals, in all the cases enumerated, as to law and fact; the judges are to decide the law and try the fact, and the trial of the fact being assigned to the judges by the constitution, a jury for trying the fact is excluded; however, under the exceptions and powers to make regulations, congress may, perhaps, introduce the jury, to try the fact in most necessary cases.

There can be but one supreme court in which the final jurisdiction will center in all federal cases—except in cases where appeals by law shall not be allowed: The judicial powers of the federal courts extend in law and equity to certain cases: and, therefore, the powers to determine on the law, in equity, and as to the fact, all will concenter in the supreme court. These powers, which by this constitution are blended in the same hands, the same judges, are in Great Britain deposited in different hands—to wit, the decision of the law in the law judges, the decision in equity in the chancellor, and the trial of the fact in the jury. It is a very dangerous thing to vest in the same judge power to decide on the law, and also general powers in equity; for if the law restrain him, he is only to step into his shoes of equity, and give what judgment his reason or opinion may dictate; we have no precedents in this country, as yet, to regulate the divisions in equity as in Great Britain; equity, therefore, in the supreme court for many years, will be mere discretion. I confess in the constitution of this supreme court, as left by the constitution, I do not see a spark of freedom or a shadow of our own or the British common law.

This court is to have appellate jurisdiction in all the other cases before mentioned: Many sensible men suppose that cases before mentioned respect, as well the criminal cases, as the civil ones, mentioned antecedently in the constitution; if so an appeal is allowed in criminal cases—contrary to the usual sense of law. How far it may be proper to admit a foreigner or the citizen of another state to bring actions against state governments, which have failed in performing so many promises made during the war, is doubtful: How far it may be proper so to humble a state, as to oblige it to answer to an individual in a court of law, is worthy of consideration; the states are now subject to no such actions; and this new jurisdiction will subject the states, and many defendants, to actions and processes, which were not in the contemplation of the parties, when the contract was made; all engagements existing between citizens of different states, citizens and foreigners, states and foreigners; and states and citizens of other states were made the parties contemplating the remedies then existing on the laws of the states—and the new remedy proposed to be given in the federal courts, can be founded on no principle whatever.

Yours Etc.

The Federal Farmer

LETTER IV

October 12, 1787.

Dear Sir,

It will not be possible to establish in the federal courts the jury trial of the vicinage so well as in the state courts.

Third. There appears to me to be not only a premature deposit of some important powers in the general government—but many of those deposited there are undefined, and may be used to good or bad purposes as honest or designing men shall prevail. By art. 1. sect. 2. representatives and direct taxes shall be apportioned among the several states, etc.—same art. sect. 8. the congress shall have powers to lay and collect taxes, duties, etc. for the common defense and general welfare, but all duties, imposts and excises, shall be uniform throughout the United States. By the first recited clause, direct taxes shall be apportioned on the states. This seems to favor the idea suggested by some sensible men and writers that congress, as to direct taxes, will only have power to make requisitions; but the latter clause, power to lay and collect taxes, etc. seems clearly to favor the contrary opinion and, in my mind, the true one, that congress shall have power to tax immediately individuals, without the intervention of the state legislatures; in fact the first clause appears to me only to provide that each state shall pay a certain portion of the tax, and the latter to provide that congress shall have power to lay and collect taxes, that is to assess upon, and to collect of the individuals in the state, the state's quota; but these, still, I consider as undefined powers, because judicious men understand them differently.

It is doubtful whether the vice-president is to have any qualifications; none are mentioned; but he may serve as president, and it may be inferred, he ought to be qualified therefore as the president; but the qualifications of the president are required only of the person to be elected president. By art. 2. sect. 2. "But the congress may by law vest the appointment of such inferior officers as they think proper in the president alone, in the courts of law, or in the heads of the departments": Who are inferior officers? May not a congress disposed to vest the appointment of all officers in the president, under this clause, vest the appointment of almost every officer in the president alone, and destroy the check mentioned in the first part of the clause, and lodged in the senate? It is true, this check is badly lodged, but then some check upon the first magistrate in appointing officers, ought, it appears by the opinion of the convention, and by the general opinion, to be established in the constitution. By art. 3. sect. 2. the supreme court shall have appellate jurisdiction as to law and facts with such exceptions, etc. to what extent is it intended the exceptions shall be carried—Congress may carry them so far as to annihilate substantially the appellate jurisdiction, and the clause be rendered of very little importance.

4th. There are certain rights which we have always held sacred in the United States, and recognized in all our constitutions, and which, by the adoption of the new constitution in its present form, will be left unsecured. By article 6, the proposed constitution, and the laws of the United States, which shall be made in pursuance thereof; and all treaties made, or which shall be made under the authority of the United States, shall be the supreme law of the land; and the judges in every state shall be bound thereby; any thing in the constitution or laws of any state to the contrary notwithstanding.

It is to be observed that when the people shall adopt the proposed constitution it will be their last and supreme act; it will be adopted not by the people of New Hampshire, Massachusetts, etc. but by the people of the United States; and wherever this constitution, or any part of it, shall be incompatible with the ancient customs, rights, the laws or the constitutions heretofore established in the United States, it will entirely abolish them and do them away: And not only this, but the laws of the United States which shall be made in pursuance of the federal constitution will be also supreme laws, and wherever they shall be incompatible with those customs, rights, laws or constitutions heretofore established, they will also entirely abolish them and do them away.

By the article before recited, treaties also made under the authority of the United States, shall be the supreme law. It is not said that these treaties shall be made in pursuance of the constitution—nor are there any constitutional bounds set to those who shall make them: The president and two-thirds of the senate will be empowered to make treaties indefinitely, and when these treaties shall be made, they will also abolish all laws and state constitutions incompatible with them. This power in the president and senate is absolute, and the judges will be bound to allow full force to whatever rule, article or thing the president and senate shall establish by treaty. Whether it be practicable to set any bounds to those who make treaties, I am not able to say: if not, it proves that this power ought to be more safely lodged.

The federal constitution, the laws of congress made in pursuance of the constitution, and all treaties must have full force and effect in all parts of the United States; and all other laws, rights and constitutions which stand in their way must yield: It is proper the national laws should be supreme, and superior to state or district laws: but then the national laws ought to yield to inalienable or fundamental rights—and national laws, made by a few men, should extend only to a few national objects. This will not be the case with the laws of congress: To have any proper idea of their extent, we must carefully examine the legislative, executive and judicial powers proposed to be lodged in the general government, and consider them in connection with a general clause in art. 1. sect. 8. in these words (after enumerating a number of powers) "To make all laws which shall be necessary and proper for carrying into execution the foregoing powers, and all other powers vested by this constitution in the government of the United States, or in any department or officer thereof." The powers of this government as has been observed, extend to internal as well as external objects, and to those objects to which all others are subordinate: it is almost impossible to have a just conception of these powers, or of the extent and number of the laws which may be deemed necessary and proper to carry them into effect, till we shall come to exercise those powers and make the laws. In making laws to carry those powers into effect, it is to be expected, that a wise and prudent congress will pay respect to the opinions of a free people, and bottom their laws on those principles which have been considered as essential and fundamental in the British, and in our government: But a congress of a different character will not be bound by the constitution to pay respect to those principles.

It is said, that when the people make a constitution, and delegate powers, that all powers not delegated by them to those who govern, is reserved in the people; and that the people, in the present case, have reserved in themselves, and in their state governments, every right and power not expressly given by the federal constitution to those who shall administer the national government. It is said, on the other hand, that the people, when they make a constitution, yield all power not expressly reserved to themselves. The truth is, in either case, it is mere matter of opinion, and men usually take either side of the argument, as will best answer their purposes: But the general presumption being, that men who govern, will, in doubtful cases, construe laws and constitutions most favorably for increasing their own powers; all wise and prudent people, in forming constitutions, have drawn the line, and carefully described the powers parted with and the powers reserved. By the state constitutions, certain rights have been reserved in the people; or rather, they have been recognized and established in such a manner, that state legislatures are bound to respect them, and to make no laws infringing upon them. The state legislatures are obliged to take notice of the bills of rights of their respective states. The bills of rights, and the state constitutions, are fundamental compacts only between those who govern, and the people of the same state.

In the year 1788 the people of the United States make a federal constitution, which is a fundamental compact between them and their federal rulers; these rulers, in the nature of things, cannot be bound to take notice of any other compact. It would be absurd for them, in making laws, to look over thirteen, fifteen, or twenty state constitutions, to see what rights are established as fundamental, and must not be infringed upon, in making laws in the society. It is true, they would be bound to do it if the people, in their federal compact, should refer to the state constitutions, recognize all parts not inconsistent with the federal constitution, and direct their federal rulers to take notice of them accordingly; but this is not the case, as the plan stands proposed at present; and it is absurd, to suppose so unnatural an idea is intended or implied. I think my opinion is not only founded in reason, but I think it is supported by the report of the convention itself. If there are a number of rights established by the state constitutions, and which will remain sacred, and the general government is bound to take notice of them—it must take notice of one as well as another; and if unnecessary to recognize or establish one by the federal constitution, it would be unnecessary to recognize or establish another by it. If the federal constitution is to be construed so far in connection with the state constitutions, as to leave the trial by jury in civil cases, for instance, secured; on the same principles it would have left the trial by jury in criminal cases, the benefits of the writ of habeas corpus, etc. secured; they all stand on the same footing; they are the common rights of Americans, and have been recognized by the state constitutions: But the convention found it necessary to recognize or re-establish the benefits of that writ, and the jury trial in criminal cases. As to *expost facto* laws, the convention has done the same in one case, and gone further in another. It is a part of the compact between the people of each state and their rulers, that no *expost facto* laws shall be made. But the convention, by art. 1. sect. 10. have put a sanction upon this part even of the state compacts. In fact, the 9th and 10th sections in art. 1. in the proposed constitution, are no more nor less, than a partial bill of rights; they establish certain principles as part of the compact upon which the federal legislators and officers can never infringe. It is here wisely stipulated, that the federal legislature shall never pass a bill of attainder, or *expost facto* law; that no tax shall be laid on articles exported, etc. The establishing of one right implies the necessity of establishing another and similar one.

On the whole, the position appears to me to be undeniable, that this bill of rights ought to be carried farther, and some other principles established, as a part of this fundamental compact between the people of the United States and their federal rulers.

It is true, we are not disposed to differ much, at present, about religion; but when we are making a constitution, it is to be hoped, for ages and millions yet unborn, why not establish the free exercise of religion, as a part of the national compact. There are other essential rights, which we have justly understood to be the rights of freemen; as freedom from hasty and unreasonable search warrants, warrants not founded on oath, and not issued with due caution, for searching and seizing men's papers, property, and persons. The trials by jury in civil cases, it is said, varies so much in the several states, that no words could be found for the uniform establishment of it. If so, the federal legislation will not be able to establish it by any general laws. I confess I am of opinion it may be established, but not in that beneficial manner in which we may enjoy it, for the reasons beforementioned. When I speak of the jury trial of the vicinage, or the trial of the fact in the neighborhood, I do not lay so much stress upon the circumstance of our being tried by our neighbors: in this enlightened country men may be probably impartially tried by those who do not live very near them: but the trial of facts in the neighborhood is of great importance in other respects. Nothing can be more essential than the cross examining of witnesses, and generally before the triers of the facts in question. The common people can establish facts with much more ease with oral than written evidence; when trials of facts are removed to a distance from the homes of the parties and witnesses, oral evidence becomes intolerably expensive, and the parties must depend on written evidence, which to the common people is expensive and almost useless; it must be frequently taken *ex parte*, and but very seldom leads to the proper discovery of truth.

The trial by jury is very important in another point of view. It is essential in every free country, that common people should have a part and share of influence, in the judicial as well as in the legislative department. To hold open to them the offices of senators, judges, and offices to fill which an expensive education is required, cannot answer any valuable purposes for them; they are not in a situation to be brought forward and to fill those offices; these, and most other offices of any considerable importance, will be occupied by the few. The few, the well born, etc. as Mr. Adams calls them, in judicial decisions as well as in legislation, are generally disposed, and very naturally too, to favor those of their own description.

The trial by jury in the judicial department, and the collection of the people by their representatives in the legislature, are those fortunate inventions which have procured for them, in this country, their true proportion of influence, and the wisest and most fit means of protecting themselves in the community. Their situation, as jurors and representatives, enables them to acquire information and knowledge in the affairs and government of the society; and to come forward, in turn, as the sentinels and guardians of each other. I am very sorry that even a few of our countrymen should consider jurors and representatives in a different point of view, as ignorant troublesome bodies, which ought not to have any share in the concerns of government.

I confess I do not see in what cases the congress can, with any pretense of right, make a law to suppress the freedom of the press; though I am not clear, that congress is restrained from laying any duties whatever on printing, and from laying duties particularly heavy on certain pieces printed, and perhaps congress may require large bonds for the payment of these duties. Should the printer say, the freedom of the press was secured by the constitution of the state in which he lived, congress might, and perhaps, with great propriety, answer, that the federal constitution is the only compact existing between them and the people; in this compact the people have named no others, and therefore congress, in exercising the powers assigned them, and in making laws to carry them into execution, are restrained by nothing beside the federal constitution, any more than a state legislature is restrained by a compact between the magistrates and people of a county, city, or town of which the people, in forming the state constitution, have taken no notice.

It is not my object to enumerate rights of inconsiderable importance; but there are others, no doubt, which ought to be established as a fundamental part of the national system.

It is worthy observation, that all treaties are made by foreign nations with a confederacy of thirteen states—that the western country is attached to thirteen states—thirteen states have jointly and severally engaged to pay the public debts. Should a new government be formed of nine, ten, eleven, or twelve states, those treaties could not be considered as binding on the foreign nations who made them. However, I believe the probability to be, that if nine states adopt the constitution, the others will.

It may also be worthy our examination, how far the provision for amending this plan, when it shall be adopted, is of any importance. No measures can be taken towards amendments, unless two-thirds of the congress, or two-thirds of the legislatures of the several states shall agree—While power is in the hands of the people, or democratic part of the community, more especially as at present, it is easy, according to the general course of human affairs, for the few influential men in the community, to obtain conventions, alterations in government, and to persuade the common people they may change for the better, and to get from them a part of the power: But when power is once transferred from the many to the few, all changes become extremely difficult; the government, in this case, being beneficial to the few, they will be exceedingly artful and adroit in preventing any measures which may lead to a change; and nothing will produce it, but great exertions and severe struggles on the part of the common people. Every man of reflection must see, that the change now proposed, is a transfer of power from the many to the few, and the probability is, the artful and ever active aristocracy, will prevent all peaceable measures for changes, unless when they shall discover some favorable moment to increase their own influence. I am sensible, thousands of men in the United States, are disposed to adopt the proposed constitution, though they perceive it to be essentially defective, under an idea that amendments of it, may be obtained when necessary. This is a pernicious idea, it argues a servility of character totally unfit for the support of free government; it is very repugnant to that perpetual jealousy respecting liberty, so absolutely necessary in all free states, spoken of by Mr. Dickinson. However, if our countrymen are so soon changed, and the language of 1774, is become odious to them, it will be in vain to use the language of freedom, or to attempt to rouse them to free enquiries: But I shall never believe this is the case with them, whatever present appearances may be, till I shall have very strong evidence indeed of it.

Yours Etc.

The Federal Farmer

LETTER V

OCTOBER 13, 1787.

Dear Sir,

Thus I have examined the federal constitution as far as a few days leisure would permit. It opens to my mind a new scene; instead of seeing powers cautiously lodged in the hands of numerous legislators, and many magistrates, we see all important powers collecting in one center, where a few men will possess them almost at discretion. And instead of checks in the formation of the government, to secure the rights of the people against the usurpations of those they appoint to govern, we are to understand the equal division of lands among our people, and the strong arm furnished them by nature and situation, are to secure them against those usurpations. If there are advantages in the equal division of our lands, and the strong and manly habits of our people, we ought to establish governments calculated to give duration to them, and not governments which never can work naturally, till that equality of property, and those free and manly habits shall be destroyed; these evidently are not the natural basis of the proposed constitution. No man of reflection, and skilled in the science of government, can suppose these will move on harmoniously together for ages, or even for fifty years. As to the little circumstances commented upon, by some writers, with applause—as the age of a representative, of the president, etc.—they have, in my mind, no weight in the general tendency of the system.

There are, however, in my opinion, many good things in the proposed system. It is founded on elective principles, and the deposits of powers in different hands, is essentially right. The guards against those evils we have experienced in some states in legislation are valuable indeed; but the value of every feature in this system is vastly lessened for the want of that one important feature in a free government, a representation of the people. Because we have sometimes abused democracy, I am not among those men who think a democratic branch a nuisance; which branch shall be sufficiently numerous to admit some of the best informed men of each order in the community into the administration of government.

While the radical defects in the proposed system are not so soon discovered, some temptations to each state, and to many classes of men to adopt it, are very visible. It uses the democratic language of several of the state constitutions, particularly that of Massachusetts; the eastern states will receive advantages so far as the regulation of trade, by a bare majority, is committed to it: Connecticut and New Jersey will receive their share of a general impost: The middle states will receive the advantages surrounding the seat of government: The southern states will receive protection, and have their negroes represented in the legislature, and large back countries will soon have a majority in it. This system promises a large field of employment to military gentlemen, and gentlemen of the law; and in case the government shall be executed without convulsions, it will afford security to creditors, to the clergy, salary-men and others depending on money payments. So far as the system promises justice and reasonable advantages, in these respects, it ought to be supported by all honest men; but whenever it promises unequal and improper advantages to any particular states, or orders of men, it ought to be opposed.

I have, in the course of these letters observed, that there are many good things in the proposed constitution, and I have endeavored to point out many important defects in it. I have admitted that we want a federal system—that we have a system presented, which, with several alterations may be made a tolerable good one—I have admitted there is a well founded uneasiness among creditors and mercantile men. In this situation of things, you ask me what I think ought to be done? My opinion in this case is only the opinion of an individual, and so far only as it corresponds with the opinions of the honest and substantial part of the community, is it entitled to consideration. Though I am fully satisfied that the state conventions ought most seriously to direct their exertions to altering and amending the system proposed before they shall adopt it—yet I have not sufficiently examined the subject, or formed an opinion, how far it will be practicable for those conventions to carry their amendments. As to the idea, that it will be in vain for those conventions to attempt amendments, it cannot be admitted; it is impossible to say whether they can or not until the attempt shall be made; and when it shall be determined, by experience, that the conventions cannot agree in amendments, it will then be an important question before the people of the United States, whether they will adopt or not the system proposed in its present form. This subject of consolidating the states is new; and because forty or fifty men have agreed in a system, to suppose the good sense of this country, an enlightened nation, must adopt it without examination, and though in a state of profound peace, without endeavoring to amend those parts they perceive are defective, dangerous to freedom, and destructive of the valuable principles of republican government—is truly humiliating. It is true there may be danger in delay; but there is danger in adopting the system in its present form; and I see the danger in either case will arise principally from the conduct and views of two very unprincipled parties in the United States—two fires, between which the honest and substantial people have long found themselves situated. One party is composed of little insurgents, men in debt, who want no law, and who want a share of the property of others; these are called levellers, Shayites, etc. The other party is composed of a few, but more dangerous men, with their servile dependents; these avariciously grasp at all power and property; you may discover in all the actions of these men, an evident dislike to free and equal government, and they will go systematically to work to change, essentially, the forms of government in this country; these are called aristocrats, Morrisites, etc. etc. Between these two parties is the weight of the community; the men of middling property, men not in debt on the one hand, and men, on the other, content with republican governments, and not aiming at immense fortunes, offices, and power. In 1786, the little insurgents, the levellers, came forth, invaded the rights of others, and attempted to establish governments according to their wills. Their movements evidently gave encouragement to the other party, which, in 1787, has taken the political field, and with its fashionable dependents, and the tongue and the pen, is endeavouring to establish, in great haste, a politer kind of government. These two parties, which will probably be opposed or united as it may suit their interests and views, are really insignificant, compared with the solid, free, and independent part of the community. It is not my intention to suggest, that either of these parties, and the real friends of the proposed constitution, are the same men. The fact is, these aristocrats support and hasten the adoption of the proposed constitution, merely because they think it is a stepping stone to their favorite object. I think I am well founded in this idea; I think the general politics of these men support it, as well as the common observation among them, that the proffered plan is the best that can be got at present, it will do for a few years and lead to something better. The sensible and judicious part of the community will carefully weigh all these circumstances; they will view the late convention as a respectable assembly of men—America probably never will see an assembly of men of a like number, more respectable. But the members of the convention met without knowing the sentiments of one man in ten thousand in these states, respecting the new ground taken. Their doings are but the first attempts in the most important scene ever opened. Though each individual in the state conventions will not, probably, be so respectable as each individual in the federal convention, yet as the state conventions will probably consist of fifteen hundred or two thousand men of abilities, and versed in the science of government, collected from all parts of the community and from all orders of men, it must be acknowledged that the weight of respectability will be in them—In them will be collected the solid sense and the real political character of the country. Being revisers of the subject, they will possess peculiar advantages. To say that these conventions ought not to attempt, coolly and deliberately, the revision of the system, or that they cannot amend it, is very foolish or very assuming. If these conventions, after examining the system, adopt it, I shall be perfectly satisfied, and wish to see men make the administration of the government an equal blessing to all orders of men. I believe the great body of our people to be virtuous and friendly to good government, to the protection of liberty and property; and it is the duty of all good men, especially of those who are placed as sentinels to guard their rights—it is their duty to examine into the prevailing politics of parties, and to disclose them—while they avoid exciting undue suspicions, to lay facts before the people, which will enable them to form a proper judgment. Men who wish the people of this country to determine for themselves, and deliberately to fit the government to their situation, must feel some degree of indignation at those attempts to hurry the adoption of a system, and to shut the door against examination. The very attempts create suspicions, that those who make them have secret views, or see some defects in the system, which, in the hurry of affairs, they expect will escape the eye of a free people.

What can be the views of those gentlemen in Pennsylvania, who precipitated decisions on this subject? What can be the views of those gentlemen in Boston, who countenanced the printers in shutting up the press against a fair and free investigation of this important system in the usual way? The members of the convention have done their duty—why should some of them fly to their states—almost forget a propriety of behavior, and precipitate measures for the adoption of a system of their own making? I confess candidly, when I consider these circumstances in connection with the unguarded parts of the system I have mentioned, I feel disposed to proceed with very great caution, and to pay more attention than usual to the conduct of particular characters. If the constitution presented be a good one, it will stand the test with a well informed people; all are agreed there shall be state conventions to examine it; and we must believe it will be adopted, unless we suppose it is a bad one, or that those conventions will make false divisions respecting it. I admit improper measures are taken against the adoption of the system as well as for it—all who object to the plan proposed ought to point out the defects objected to, and to propose those amendments with which they can accept it, or to propose some other system of government, that the public mind may be known, and that we may be brought to agree in some system of government, to strengthen and execute the present, or to provide a substitute. I consider the field of enquiry just opened, and that we are to look to the state conventions for ultimate decisions on the subject before us; it is not to be presumed, that they will differ about small amendments, and lose a system when they shall have made it substantially good; but touching the essential amendments, it is to be presumed the several conventions will pursue the most rational measures to agree in and obtain them; and such defects as they shall discover and not remove, they will probably notice, keep them in view as the groundwork of future amendments, and in the firm and manly language which every free people ought to use, will suggest to those who may hereafter administer the government, that it is their expectation, that the system will be so organized by legislative acts, and the government so administered, as to render those defects as little injurious as possible. Our countrymen are entitled to an honest and faithful government; to a government of laws and not of men; and also to one of their choosing—as a citizen of the country, I wish to see these objects secured, and licentious, assuming, and overbearing men restrained; if the constitution or social compact be vague and unguarded, then we depend wholly upon the prudence, wisdom and moderation of those who manage the affairs of government; or on what, probably, is equally uncertain and precarious, the success of the people opposed by the abuse of government, in receiving it from the hands of those who abuse it, and placing it in the hands of those who will use it well.

In every point of view, therefore, in which I have been able, as yet, to contemplate this subject, I can discern but one rational mode of proceeding relative to it: and that is to examine it with freedom and candor, to have state conventions some months hence, which shall examine coolly every article, clause, and word in the system proposed, and to adopt it with such amendments as they shall think fit. How far the state conventions ought to pursue the mode prescribed by the federal convention of adopting or rejecting the plan in toto, I leave it to them to determine. Our examination of the subject hitherto has been rather of a general nature. The republican characters in the several states, who wish to make this plan more adequate to security of liberty and property, and to the duration of the principles of a free government, will, no doubt, collect their opinions to certain points, and accurately define those alterations and amendments they wish; if it shall be found they essentially disagree in them, the conventions will then be able to determine whether to adopt the plan as it is, or what will be proper to be done.

Under these impressions, and keeping in view the improper and unadvisable lodgment of powers in the general government, organized as it at present is, touching internal taxes, armies and militia, the elections of its own members, causes between citizens of different states, etc. and the want of a more perfect bill of rights, etc. I drop the subject for the present, and when I shall have leisure to revise and correct my ideas respecting it, and to collect into points the opinions of those who wish to make the system more secure and safe, perhaps I may proceed to point out particularly for your consideration, the amendments which ought to be ingrafted into this system, not only in conformity to my own, but the deliberate opinions of others—you will with me perceive, that the objections to the plan proposed may, by a more leisurely examination be set in a stronger point of view, especially the important one, that there is no substantial representation of the people provided for in a government in which the most essential powers, even as to the internal police of the country, are proposed to be lodged.

I think the honest and substantial part of the community will wish to see this system altered, permanency and consistency given to the constitution we shall adopt, and therefore they will be anxious to apportion the powers to the features and organization of the government, and to see abuse in the exercise of power more effectually guarded against. It is suggested, that state officers, from interested motives will oppose the constitution presented—I see no reason for this, their places in general will not be affected, but new openings to offices and places of profit must evidently be made by the adoption of the constitution in its present form.

Yours Etc.

The Federal Farmer

LETTER VI

December 25, 1787.

Dear Sir,

My former letters to you, respecting the constitution proposed, were calculated merely to lead to a fuller investigation of the subject; having more extensively considered it, and the opinions of others relative to it, I shall, in a few letters, more particularly endeavor to point out the defects, and propose amendments. I shall in this make only a few general and introductory observations, which, in the present state of the momentous question, may not be improper; and I leave you, in all cases, to decide by a careful examination of my works, upon the weight of my arguments, the propriety of my remarks, the uprightness of my intentions, and the extent of my candor—I presume I am writing to a man of candor and reflection, and not to an ardent, peevish, or impatient man.

When the constitution was first published, there appeared to prevail a misguided zeal to prevent a fair unbiased examination of a subject of infinite importance to this people and their posterity—to the cause of liberty and the rights of mankind—and it was the duty of those who saw a restless ardor, or design, attempting to mislead the people by a parade of names and misrepresentations, to endeavor to prevent their having their intended effects. The only way to stop the passions of men in their career is, coolly to state facts, and deliberately to avow the truth—and to do this we are frequently forced into a painful view of men and measures.

Since I wrote to you in October, I have heard much said, and seen many pieces written, upon the subject in question; and on carefully examining them on both sides, I find much less reason for changing my sentiments, respecting the good and defective parts of the system proposed than I expected—The opposers, as well as the advocates of it, confirm me in my opinion, that this system affords, all circumstances considered, a better basis to build upon than the confederation. And as to the principal defects, as the smallness of the representation, the insecurity of elections, the undue mixture of powers in the senate, the insecurity of some essential rights, etc. the opposition appears, generally, to agree respecting them, and many of the ablest advocates virtually to admit them—Clear it is, the latter do not attempt manfully to defend these defective parts, but to cover them with a mysterious veil; they concede, they retract; they say we could do no better; and some of them, when a little out of temper, and hard pushed, use arguments that do more honor to their ingenuity, than to their candor and firmness.

Three states have now adopted the constitution without amendments; these, and other circumstances, ought to have their weight in deciding the question, whether we will put the system into operation, adopt it, enumerate and recommend the necessary amendments, which afterwards, by three-fourths of the states, may be ingrafted into the system, or whether we will make amendments prior to the adoption—I only undertake to show amendments are essential and necessary—how far it is practicable to ingraft them into the plan, prior to the adoption, the state conventions must determine. Our situation is critical, and we have but our choice of evils—We may hazard much by adopting the constitution in its present form—we may hazard more by rejecting it wholly—we may hazard much by long contending about amendments prior to the adoption. The greatest political evils that can befall us, are discords and civil wars—the greatest blessings we can wish for, are peace, union, and industry, under a mild, free, and steady government. Amendments recommended will tend to guard and direct the administration—but there will be danger that the people, after the system shall be adopted, will become inattentive to amendments—Their attention is now awake—the discussion of the subject, which has already taken place, has had a happy effect—it has called forth the able advocates of liberty, and tends to renew, in the minds of the people, their true republican jealousy and vigilance, the strongest guard against the abuses of power; but the vigilance of the people is not sufficiently constant to be depended on—Fortunate it is for the body of a people, if they can continue attentive to their liberties, long enough to erect for them a temple, and constitutional barriers for their permanent security: when they are well fixed between the powers of the rulers and the rights of the people, they become visible boundaries, constantly seen by all, and any transgression of them is immediately discovered: they serve as sentinels for the people at all times, and especially in those unavoidable intervals of inattention.

Some of the advocates, I believe, will agree to recommend *good* amendments: but some of them will only consent to recommend indefinite, specious, but unimportant ones; and this only with a view to keep the door open for obtaining, in some favorable moment, their main object, a complete consolidation of the states, and a government much higher toned, less republican and free than the one proposed. If necessity, therefore, should ever oblige us to adopt the system, and recommend amendments, the true friends of a federal republic must see they are well defined, and well calculated, not only to prevent our system of government moving further from republican principles and equality, but to bring it back nearer to them—they must be constantly on their guard against the address, flattery, and maneuvers of their adversaries.

The gentlemen who oppose the constitution, or contend for amendments in it, are frequently, and with much bitterness, charged with wantonly attacking the men who framed it. The unjustness of this charge leads me to make one observation upon the conduct of parties, etc. Some of the advocates are only pretended federalists; in fact they wish for an abolition of the state governments. Some of them I believe to be honest federalists, who wish to preserve *substantially* the state governments united under an efficient federal head; and many of them are blind tools without any object. Some of the opposers also are only pretended federalists, who want no federal government, or one merely advisory. Some of them are the true federalists, their object, perhaps, more clearly seen, is the same with that of the honest federalists; and some of them, probably, have no distinct object. We might as well call the advocates and opposers tories and whigs, or any thing else, as federalists and anti-federalists. To be for or against the constitution, as it stands, is not much evidence of a federal disposition; if any names are applicable to the parties, on account of their general politics, they are those of republicans and anti-republicans. The opposers are generally men who support the rights of the body of the people, and are properly republicans. The advocates are generally men not very friendly to those rights, and properly anti-republicans.

Had the advocates left the constitution, as they ought to have done, to be adopted or rejected on account of its own merits or imperfections, I do not believe the gentlemen who framed it would ever have been even alluded to in the contest by the opposers. Instead of this, the ardent advocates began by quoting names as incontestible authorities for the implicit adoption of the system, without any examination—treated all who opposed it as friends of anarchy: and with an indecent virulence addressed M——n, G——y, L——e [this refers to George Mason of Virginia, Elbridge Gerry of Massachusetts, and Lee himself. Mason and Gerry were both in the Constitutional Convention, refused to sign the Constitution, and fought ratification], and almost every man of weight they could find in the opposition by name. If they had been candid men they would have applauded the moderation of the opposers for not retaliating in this pointed manner, when so fair an opportunity was given them; but the opposers generally saw that it was no time to heat the passions; but, at the same time, they saw there was something more than mere zeal in many of their adversaries; they saw them attempting to mislead the people, and to precipitate their divisions, by the sound of names, and forced to do it, the opposers, in general terms, alleged those names were not of sufficient authority to justify the hasty adoption of the system contended for. The convention, as a body, was undoubtedly respectable; it was, generally, composed of members of the then and preceding congresses: as a body of respectable men we ought to view it. To select individual names, is an invitation to personal attacks, and the advocates, for their own sake, ought to have known the abilities, politics, and situation of some of their favorite characters better, before they held them up to view in the manner they did, as men entitled to our implicit political belief; they ought to have known, whether all the men they so held up to view could, for their past conduct in public offices, be approved or not by the public records, and the honest part of the community. These ardent advocates seem now to be peevish and angry, because, by their own folly, they have led to an investigation of facts and of political characters, unfavorable to them, which they had not the discernment to foresee. They may well apprehend they have opened a door to some Junius, or to some man, after his manner, with his polite addresses to men by name, to state serious facts, and unfold the truth; but these advocates may rest assured, that cool men in the opposition, best acquainted with the affairs of the country, will not, in the critical passage of a people from one constitution to another, pursue enquiries, which, in other circumstances, will be deserving of the highest praise. I will say nothing further about political characters, but examine the constitution; and as a necessary and previous measure to a particular examination, I shall state a few general positions and principles, which receive a general assent, and briefly notice the leading features of the confederation, and several state conventions, to which, through the whole investigation, we must frequently have recourse, to aid the mind in its determinations.

We can put but little dependence on the partial and vague information transmitted to us respecting ancient governments; our situation as a people is peculiar: our people in general have a high sense of freedom; they are high-spirited, though capable of deliberate measures; they are intelligent, discerning, and well informed; and it is to their condition we must mold the constitution and laws. We have no royal or noble families, and all things concur in favor of a government entirely elective. We have tried our abilities as freemen in a most arduous contest, and have succeeded; but we now find the mainspring of our movements were the love of liberty, and a temporary ardor, and not any energetic principle in the federal system.

Our territories are far too extensive for a limited monarchy, in which the representatives must frequently assemble, and the laws operate mildly and systematically. The most eligible system is a federal republic, that is, a system in which national concerns may be transacted in the center, and local affairs in state or district governments.

The powers of the union ought to be extended to commerce, the coin, and national objects; and a division of powers, and a deposit of them in different hands, is safest.

Good government is generally the result of experience and gradual improvements, and a punctual execution of the laws is essential to the preservation of life, liberty, and property. Taxes are always necessary, and the power to raise them can never be safely lodged without checks and limitation, but in a full and substantial representation of the body of the people; the quantity of power delegated ought to be compensated by the brevity of the time of holding it, in order to prevent the possessors increasing it. The supreme power is in the people, and rulers possess only that portion which is expressly given them; yet the wisest people have often declared this is the case on proper occasions, and have carefully formed stipulations to fix the extent, and limit the exercise of the power given.

The people by Magna Charta, etc. did not acquire powers, or receive privileges from the king, they only ascertained and fixed those they were entitled to as Englishmen; the title used by the king "we grant," was mere form. Representation and the jury trial are the best features of a free government ever as yet discovered, and the only means by which the body of the people can have their proper influence in the affairs of government.

In a federal system we must not only balance the parts of the same government, as that of the state, or that of the union; but we must find a balancing influence between the general and local governments—the latter is what men or writers have but very little or imperfectly considered.

A free and mild government is that in which no laws can be made without the formal and free consent of the people, or of their constitutional representatives; that is, of a substantial representative branch. Liberty, in its genuine sense, is security to enjoy the effects of our honest industry and labors, in a free and mild government, and personal security from all illegal restraints.

Of rights, some are natural and inalienable, of which even the people cannot deprive individuals: Some are constitutional or fundamental; these cannot be altered or abolished by the ordinary laws; but the people, by express acts, may alter or abolish them—These, such as the trial by jury, the benefits of the writ of habeas corpus, etc. individuals claim under the solemn compacts of the people, as constitutions, or at least under laws so strengthened by long usage as not to be repealable by the ordinary legislature—and some are common or mere legal rights, that is, such as individuals claim under laws which the ordinary legislature may alter or abolish at pleasure.

The confederation is a league of friendship among the states or sovereignties for the common defense and mutual welfare—Each state expressly retains its sovereignty, and all powers not expressly given to congress—All federal powers are lodged in a congress of delegates annually elected by the state legislatures, except in Connecticut and Rhode Island, where they are chosen by the people—Each state has a vote in congress, pays its delegates, and may instruct or recall them; no delegate can hold any office of profit, or serve more than three years in any six years—Each state may be represented by not less than two, or more than seven delegates.

Congress (nine states agreeing) may make peace and war, treaties and alliances, grant letters of mark and reprisal, coin money, regulate the alloy and value of the coin, require men and monies of the states by fixed proportions, and appropriate monies, form armies and navies, emit bills of credit, and borrow monies.

Congress (seven states agreeing) may send and receive ambassadors, regulate captures, make rules for governing the army and navy, institute courts for the trial of piracies and felonies committed on the high seas, and for settling territorial disputes between the individual states, regulate weight and measures, post offices, and Indian affairs.

No state, without the consent of congress, can send or receive embassies, make any agreement with any other state, or a foreign state, keep up any vessels of war or bodies of forces in time of peace, or engage in war, or lay any duties which may interfere with the treaties of congress—Each state must appoint regimental officers, and keep up a well regulated militia—Each state may prohibit the importation or exportation of any species of goods.

The free inhabitants of one state are entitled to the privileges and immunities of the free citizens of the other states—Credit in each state shall be given to the records and judicial proceedings in the others.

Canada, acceding, may be admitted, and any other colony may be admitted, by the consent of nine states.

Alterations may be made by the agreement of congress, and confirmation of all the state legislatures.

The following, I think, will be allowed to be inalienable or fundamental rights in the United States:

No man, demeaning himself peaceably, shall be molested on account of his religion or mode of worship—The people have a right to hold and enjoy their property according to known standing laws, and which cannot be taken from them without their consent, or the consent of their representatives; and whenever taken in the pressing urgencies of government, they are to receive a reasonable compensation for it—Individual security consists in having free recourse to the laws—The people are subject to no laws or taxes not assented to by their representatives constitutionally assembled—They are at all times entitled to the benefits of the writ of habeas corpus, the trial by jury in criminal and civil cases—They have a right, when charged, to a speedy trial in the vicinage; to be heard by themselves or counsel, not to be compelled to furnish evidence against themselves, to have witnesses face to face, and to confront their adversaries before the judge—No man is held to answer a crime charged upon him till it be substantially described to him; and he is subject to no unreasonable searches or seizures of his person, papers or effects—The people have a right to assemble in an orderly manner, and petition the government for a redress of wrongs—The freedom of the press ought not to be restrained—No emoluments, except for actual service—No hereditary honors, or orders of nobility, ought to be allowed—The military ought to be subordinate to the civil authority, and no solider be quartered on the citizens without their consent—The militia ought always to be armed and disciplined, and the usual defense of the country—The supreme power is in the people, and power delegated ought to return to them at stated periods, and frequently—The legislative, executive, and judicial powers, ought always to be kept distinct—others perhaps might be added.

The organization of the state governments—Each state has a legislature, an executive, and a judicial branch—In general legislators are excluded from the important executive and judicial offices—Except in the Carolinas there is no constitutional distinction among Christian sects—The constitution of New York, Delaware, and

Virginia, exclude the clergy from offices civil and military—the other states do nearly the same in practice.

Each state has a democratic branch, elected twice a year in Rhode Island and Connecticut, biennially in South Carolina, and annually in the other states—There are about 1500 representatives in all the states, or one to each 1700 inhabitants, reckoning five blacks for three whites—The states do not differ as to the age or moral characters of the electors or elected, nor materially as to their property.

Pennsylvania has lodged all her legislative powers in a single branch, and Georgia has done the same; the other eleven states have each in their legislatures a second or senatorial branch. In forming this they have combined various principles, and aimed at several checks and balances. It is amazing to see how ingenuity has worked in the several states to fix a barrier against popular instability. In Massachusetts the senators are apportioned in districts according to the taxes they pay, nearly according to property. In Connecticut the freemen, in September, vote for twenty counsellers, and return the names of those voted for in the several towns; the legislature takes the twenty who have the most votes, and give them to the people, who, in April, choose twelve of them, who, with the governor and deputy governor, form the senatorial branch. In Maryland the senators are chosen by two electors from each county; these electors are chosen by the freemen, and qualified as the members in the democratic branch are: In these two cases checks are aimed at in the mode of election. Several states have taken into view the periods of service, age, property, etc. In South Carolina a senator is elected for two years, in Delaware three, and in New York and Virginia four, in Maryland five, and in the other states for one. In New York and Virginia one-fourth part go out yearly. In Virginia a senator must be twenty-five years old, in South Carolina thirty. In New York the electors must each have a freehold worth 250 dollars, in North Carolina a freehold of fifty acres of land; in the other states the electors of senators are qualified as electors of representatives are. In Massachusetts a senator must have a freehold in his own right worth 1000 dollars, or any estate worth 2000, in New Jersey any estate worth 2666, in South Carolina worth 1300 dollars, in North Carolina 300 acres of land in fee, etc. The numbers of senators in each state are from ten to thirty-one, about 160 in the eleven states, about one to 14,000 inhabitants.

Two states, Massachusetts and New York, have each introduced into their legislatures a third, but incomplete branch. In the former, the governor may negative any law not supported by two-thirds of the senators, and two-thirds of the representatives: in the latter, the governor, chancellor, and judges of the supreme court may do the same.

Each state has a single executive branch. In the five eastern states the people at large elect their governors; in the other states the legislatures elect them. In South Carolina the governor is elected once in two years; in New York and Delaware once in three, and in the other states annually. The governor of New York has no executive council, the other governors have. In several states the governor has a vote in the senatorial branch—the governors have similar powers in some instances, and quite dissimilar ones in others. The number of executive counsellers in the states are from five to twelve. In the four eastern states, New Jersey, Pennsylvania, and Georgia, they are of the men returned legislators by the people. In Pennsylvania the counsellers are chosen triennially, in Delaware every fourth year, in Virginia every three years, in South Carolina biennially, and in the other states yearly.

Each state has a judicial branch; each common law courts, superior and inferior; some chancery and admiralty courts: The courts in general sit in different places, in order to accommodate the citizens. The trial by jury is had in all the common law courts, and in some of the admiralty courts. The democratic freemen principally form the juries; men destitute of property, of character, or under age, are excluded as in elections. Some of the judges are during good behavior, and some appointed for a year, and some for years; and all are dependent on the legislatures for their salaries—Particulars respecting this department are too many to be noticed here.

The Federal Farmer

LETTER VII

December 31, 1787.

Dear Sir,

In viewing the various governments instituted by mankind, we see their whole force reducible to two principles—the important springs which alone move the machines, and give them their intended influence and control, are force and persuasion: by the former men are compelled, by the latter they are drawn. We denominate a government despotic or free, as the one or other principle prevails in it. Perhaps it is not possible for a government to be so despotic, as not to operate persuasively on some of its subjects; nor is it, in the nature of things, I conceive, for a government to be so free, or so supported by voluntary consent, as never to want force to compel obedience to the laws. In despotic governments one man, or a few men, independent of the people, generally make the laws, command obedience, and enforce it by the sword: one-fourth part of the people are armed, and obliged to endure the fatigues of soldiers, to oppress the others and keep them subject to the laws. In free governments the people, or their representatives, make the laws; their execution is principally the effect of voluntary consent and aid; the people respect the magistrate, follow their private pursuits, and enjoy the fruits of their labor with very small deductions for the public use. The body of the people must evidently prefer the latter species of government; and it can be only those few who may be well paid for the part they take in enforcing despotism, that can, for a moment, prefer the former. Our true object is to give full efficacy to one principle, to arm persuasion on every side, and to render force as little necessary as possible. Persuasion is never dangerous, not even in despotic governments; but military force, if often applied internally, can never fail to destroy the love and confidence, and break the spirits, of the people: and to render it totally impracticable and unnatural for him or them who govern, and yield to this force against the people, to hold their places by the peoples' elections.

I repeat my observation, that the plan proposed will have a doubtful operation between the two principles; and whether it will preponderate towards persuasion or force is uncertain.

Government must exist—If the persuasive principle be feeble, force is infallibly the next resort. The moment the laws of congress shall be disregarded they must languish, and the whole system be convulsed—that moment we must have recourse to this next resort, and all freedom vanish.

It being impracticable for the people to assemble to make laws, they must elect legislators, and assign men to the different departments of the government. In the representative branch we must expect chiefly to collect the confidence of the people, and in it to find almost entirely the force of persuasion. In forming this branch, therefore, several important considerations must be attended to. It must possess abilities to discern the situation of the people and of public affairs, a disposition to sympathize with the people, and a capacity and inclination to make laws congenial to their circumstances and condition: it must afford security against interested combinations, corruption and influence; it must possess the confidence, and have the voluntary support of the people.

I think these positions will not be controverted, nor the one I formerly advanced, that a fair and equal representation is that in which the interests, feelings, opinions and views of the people are collected, in such manner as they would be were the people all assembled. Having made these general observations, I shall proceed to consider further my principal position, viz. that there is no substantial representation of the people provided for in a government, in which the most essential powers, even as to the internal police of the country, are proposed to be lodged; and to propose certain amendments as to the representative branch: 1st, That there ought to be *an increase of the numbers of representatives*: And, 2dly, That the elections of them ought to be better secured.

1. The representation is unsubstantial and ought to be increased. In matters where there is much room for opinion, you will not expect me to establish my positions with mathematical certainty; you must only expect my observations to be candid, and such as are well-founded in the mind of the writer. I am in a field where doctors disagree; and as to genuine representation, though no feature in government can be more important, perhaps, no one has been less understood, and no one that has received so imperfect a consideration by political writers. The ephori in Sparta, and the tribunes in Rome, were but the shadow; the representation in Great Britain is unequal and insecure. In America we have done more in establishing this important branch on its true principles, than, perhaps, all the world besides: yet even here, I conceive, that very great improvements in representation may be made. In fixing this branch, the situation of the people must be surveyed, and the number of representatives and forms of election apportioned to that situation. When we find a numerous people settled in a fertile and extensive country, possessing equality, and few or none of them oppressed with riches or wants, it ought to be the anxious care of the constitution and laws, to arrest them from national depravity, and to preserve them in their happy condition. A virtuous people make just laws, and good laws tend to preserve unchanged a virtuous people. A virtuous and happy people by laws uncongenial to their characters, may easily be gradually changed into servile and depraved creatures. Where the people, or their representatives, make the laws, it is probable they will generally be fitted to the national character and circumstances, unless the representation be partial, and the imperfect substitute of the people. However, the people may be electors, if the representation be so formed as to give one or more of the natural classes of men in the society an undue ascendency over the others, it is imperfect; the former will gradually become masters, and the latter slaves. It is the first of all among the political balances, to preserve in its proper station each of these classes. We talk of balances in the legislature, and among the departments of government; we ought to carry them to the body of the people. Since I advanced the idea of balancing the several orders of men in a community, in forming a genuine representation, and have seen that idea considered as chimerical, I have been sensibly

struck with a sentence in the Marquis Beccaria's treatise: this sentence was quoted by congress in 1774, and is as follows: "In every society there is an effort continually tending to confer on one part the height of power and happiness, and to reduce the others to the extreme of weakness and misery; the intent of good laws is to oppose this effort, and to diffuse their influence universally and equally." Add to this Montesquieu's opinion, that "in a free state every man, who is supposed to be a free agent, ought to be concerned in his own government: therefore, the legislative should reside in the whole body of the people, or their representatives." It is extremely clear that these writers had in view the several orders of men in society, which we call aristocratic, democratic, mercantile, mechanic, etc. and perceived the efforts they are constantly, from interested and ambitious views, disposed to make to elevate themselves and oppress others. Each order must have a share in the business of legislation actually and efficiently. It is deceiving a people to tell them they are electors, and can choose their legislators, if they cannot, in the nature of things, choose men from among themselves, and genuinely like themselves. I wish you to take another idea along with you; we are not only to balance these natural efforts, but we are also to guard against accidental combinations; combinations founded on the connections of offices and private interests, both evils which are increased in proportion as the number of men, among which the elected must be, are decreased. To set this matter in a proper point of view, we must form some general ideas and descriptions of the different classes of men, as they may be divided by occupations and politically: the first class is the aristocratic. There are three kinds of aristocracy spoken of in this country—the first is a constitutional one, which does not exist in the United States in our common acceptation of the word. Montesquieu, it is true, observes, that where a part of the persons in a society, for lack of property, age, or moral character, are excluded any share in the government, the others, who alone are the constitutional electors are elected, form this aristocracy; this, according to him, exists in each of the United States, where a considerable number of persons, as all convicted of crimes, underage, or not possessed of certain property, are excluded any share in the government—the second is an aristocratic faction; a junto of unprincipled men, often distinguished for their wealth or abilities, who combine together and make their object their private interests and aggrandizement; the existence of this description is merely accidental, but particularly to be guarded against. The third is the natural aristocracy; this term we use to designate a respectable order of men, the line between whom and the natural democracy is in some degree arbitrary; we may place men on one side of this line, which others may place on the other, and in all disputes between the few and the many, a considerable number are wavering and uncertain themselves on which side they are, or ought to be. In my idea of our natural aristocracy in the United States I include about four or five thousand men; and among these I reckon those who have been placed in the offices of governors, of members of Congress, and state senators generally, in the principal officers of Congress, of the army and militia, the superior judges, the most eminent professional men, etc. and men of large property—the other persons and orders in the community form the natural democracy; this includes in general the yeomanry, the subordinate officers, civil and military, the fishermen, mechanics and traders, many of the merchants and professional men. It is easy to perceive that men of these two classes, the aristocratic and democratic, with views equally honest, have sentiments widely different, especially respecting public and private expenses, salaries, taxes, etc. Men of the first class associate more extensively, have a high sense of honor, possess abilities, ambition, and general knowledge; men of the second class are not so much used to combining great objects; they possess less ambition, and a larger share of honesty; their dependence is principally on middling and small estates, industrious pursuits, and hard labor, while that of the former is principally on the emoluments of large estates, and of the chief offices of government. Not only the efforts of these two great parties are to be balanced, but other interests and parties also, which do not always oppress each other merely for want of power, and for fear of the consequences; though they, in fact, mutually depend on each other; yet such are their general views, that the merchants alone would never fail to make laws favorable to themselves and oppressive to the farmers, etc.; the farmers alone would act on like principles; the former would tax the land, the latter the trade. The manufacturers are often disposed to contend for monopolies, buyers make every exertion to lower prices, and sellers to raise them; men who live by fees and salaries endeavor to raise them, and the part of the people who pay them, endeavor to lower them; the public creditors to augment the taxes, and the people at large to lessen them. Thus, in every period of society, and in all the transactions of men, we see parties verifying the observation made by the Marquis; and those classes which have not their sentinels in the government, in proportion to what they have to gain or lose, must infallibly be ruined.

Efforts among parties are not merely confined to property; they contend for rank and distinctions; all their passions in turn are entitled in political controversies—Men, elevated in society, are often disgusted with the changeableness of the democracy, and the latter are often agitated with the passions of jealousy and envy: the yeomanry possess a large share of property and strength, are nervous and firm in their opinions and habits—the mechanics of towns are ardent and changeable, honest and credulous, they are inconsiderable in numbers, weight and strength, not always sufficiently stable for the supporting of free governments; the fishing interest partakes partly of the strength and stability of the landed, and partly of the changeableness of the mechanic interest. As to merchants and traders, they are our agents in almost all money transactions; give activity to government, and possess a considerable share of influence in it. It has been observed by an able writer, that frugal industrious merchants are generally advocates for liberty. It is an observation, I believe, well-founded, that the schools produce but few advocates for republican forms of government; gentlemen of the law, divinity, physic, etc. probably form about a fourth part of the people; yet their political influence, perhaps, is equal to that of all the other descriptions of men; if we may judge from the appointments to Congress, the legal characters will often, in a small representation, be the majority; but the more the representatives are increased, the more of the farmers, merchants, etc. will be found to be brought into the government.

These general observations will enable you to discern what I intend by different classes, and the general scope of my ideas, when I contend for uniting and balancing their interests, feelings, opinions, and views in the legislature; we may not only so unite and balance these as to prevent a change in the government by the gradual exaltation of one part to the depression of others, but we may derive many other advantages from the combination and full representation; a small representation can never be well informed as to the circumstances of the people, the members of it must be too far removed from the people, in general, to sympathize with them, and too few to communicate with them; a representation must be extremely imperfect where the representatives are not circumstanced to make the proper communications to their constituents, and where the constituents in turn cannot, with tolerable convenience, make known their wants, circumstances and opinions, to their representatives; where there is but one representative to 30,000 or 40,000 inhabitants, it appears to me, he can only mix, and be acquainted with a few respectable characters among his constituents, even double the federal representation, and then there must be a very great distance between the representatives and the people in general represented. On the proposed plan, the state of Delaware, the city of Philadelphia, the state of Rhode Island, the province of Maine, the county of Suffolk in Massachusetts will have one representative each; there can be but little personal knowledge, or but few communications, between him and the people at large of either of those districts. It has been observed, that mixing only with the respectable men, he will get the best information and ideas from them; he will also receive impressions favorable to their purposes particularly. Many plausible shifts have been made to divert the mind from dwelling on this defective representation, these I shall consider in another place.

Could we get over all our difficulties respecting a balance of interests and party efforts, to raise some and oppress others, the lack of sympathy, information and intercourse between the representatives and the people, an insuperable difficulty will still remain, I mean the constant liability of a small number of representatives to private combinations; the tyranny of the one, or the licentiousness of the multitude, are, in my mind, but small evils compared with the factions of the few. It is a consideration well worth pursuing, how far this house of representatives will be liable to be formed into private juntos, how far influenced by expectations of appointments and offices, how far liable to be managed by the president and senate, and how far the people will have confidence in them. To obviate difficulties on this head, as well as objections to the representative branch, generally, several observations have been made—these I will now examine, and if they shall appear to be unfounded, the objections must stand unanswered.

That the people are the electors, must elect good men, and attend to the administration.

It is said that the members of congress, at stated periods, must return home, and that they must be subject to the laws they may make, and to a share of the burdens they may impose.

That the people possess the strong arm to overawe their rulers, and the best checks in their national character against the abuses of power, that the supreme power will remain in them.

That the state governments will form a part of, and a balance in the system.

That congress will have only a few national objects to attend to, and the state governments many and local ones.

That the new congress will be more numerous than the present, and that any numerous body is unwieldy and mobbish.

That the states only are represented in the present congress, and that the people will require a representation in the new one; that in fifty or an hundred years the representation will be numerous.

That congress will have no temptation to do wrong; and that no system to enslave the people is practicable.

That as long as the people are free they will preserve free governments; and that when they shall become tired of freedom, arbitrary government must take place.

These observations I shall examine in the course of my letters; and, I think, not only show that they are not well-founded, but point out the fallacy of some of them; and show that others do not very well comport with the dignified and manly sentiments of a free and enlightened people.

The Federal Farmer

LETTER XVI

January 20, 1788.

Dear Sir,

Having gone through with the organization of the government, I shall now proceed to examine more particularly those clauses which respect its powers. I shall begin with those articles and stipulations which are necessary for accurately ascertaining the extent of powers, and what is given, and for guarding, limiting, and restraining them in their exercise. We often find these articles and stipulations placed in bills of rights; but they may as well be incorporated in the body of the constitution, as selected and placed by themselves. The constitution, or whole social compact, is but one instrument, no more or less than a certain number of articles or stipulations agreed to by the people, whether it consists of articles, sections, chapters, bills of rights, or parts of any other denomination, cannot be material. Many needless observations, and idle distinctions, in my opinion, have been made respecting a bill of rights. On the one hand, it seems to be considered as a necessary distinct limb of the constitution, and as containing a certain number of very valuable articles, which are applicable to all societies: and, on the other, as useless, especially in a federal government, possessing only enumerated power—nay, dangerous, as individual rights are numerous, and not easy to be enumerated in a bill of rights, and from articles, or stipulations, securing some of them, it may be inferred, that others not mentioned are surrendered. There appears to be general indefinite propositions without much meaning—and the man who first advanced those of the latter description, in the present case, signed the federal constitution, which directly contradicts him. The supreme power is undoubtedly in the people, and it is a principle well-established in my mind, that they reserve all powers not expressly delegated by them to those who govern; this is as true in forming a state as in forming a federal government.

There is no possible distinction but this founded merely in the different modes of proceeding which take place in some cases. In forming a state constitution, under which to manage not only the great but the little concerns of a community: the powers to be possessed by the government are often too numerous to be enumerated; the people to adopt the shortest way often give general powers, indeed all powers, to the government, in some general words, and then, by a particular enumeration, take back, or rather say they however reserve certain rights as sacred, and which no laws shall be made to violate: hence the idea that all powers are given which are not reserved; but in forming a federal constitution, which *ex vi termine*, supposes state governments existing, and which is only to manage a few great national concerns, we often find it easier to enumerate particularly the powers to be delegated to the federal head, than to enumerate particularly the individual rights to be reserved; and the principle will operate in its full force, when we carefully adhere to it. When we particularly enumerate the powers given, we ought either carefully to enumerate the rights reserved, or be totally silent about them; we must either particularly enumerate both, or else suppose the particular enumeration of the powers given adequately draws the line between them and the rights reserved, particularly to enumerate the former and not the latter, I think most advisable: however, as men appear generally to have their doubts about these silent reservations, we might advantageously enumerate the powers given, and then in general words, according to the mode adopted in the 2d art. of the confederation, declare all powers, rights and privileges, are reserved, which are not explicitly and expressly given up. People, and very wisely too, like to be express and explicit about their essential rights, and not to be forced to claim them on the precarious and unascertained tenure of inferences and general principles, knowing that in any controversy between them and their rulers, concerning those rights, disputes may be endless, and nothing certain—But admitting, on the general principle, that all rights are reserved of course, which are not expressly surrendered, the people could with sufficient certainty assert their rights on all occasions, and establish them with ease, still there are infinite advantages in particularly enumerating many of the most essential rights reserved in all cases; and as to the less important ones, we may declare in general terms, that all not expressly surrendered are reserved. We do not by declarations change the nature of things, or create new truths, but we give existence, or at least establish in the minds of the people truths and principles which they might never otherwise have thought of, or soon forgot. If a nation means its systems, religious or political, shall have duration, it ought to recognize the leading principles of them in the front page of every family book. What is the usefulness of a truth in theory, unless it exists constantly in the minds of the people, and has their assent: we discern certain rights, as the freedom of the press, and the trial by jury, etc. which the people of England and of America of course believe to be sacred, and essential to their political happiness, and this belief in them is the result of ideas at first suggested to them by a few able men, and of subsequent experience; while the people of some other countries hear these rights mentioned with the utmost indifference; they think the privilege of existing at the will of a despot much preferable to them. Why this difference among beings in every way formed alike? The reason of the difference is obvious—it is the effect of education, a series of notions impressed upon the minds of the people by examples, precepts and declarations. When the people of England got together, at the time they formed Magna Charta, they did not consider it sufficient, that they were indisputably entitled to certain natural and inalienable rights, not depending on silent titles, they, by a declaratory act, expressly recognized them, and explicitly declared to all the world, that they were entitled to enjoy those rights; they made an instrument in writing, and enumerated those they then thought essential, or in danger, and this wise men saw was not sufficient; and therefore, that the people might not forget these rights, and gradually become prepared for arbitrary government, their discerning and honest leaders caused this instrument to be confirmed nearly forty times, and to be read twice a year in public places, not that it would lose its validity without such confirmations, but to fix the contents of it in the minds of the people, as they successively come upon the stage. Men, in some countries do not remain free, merely because they are entitled to natural and inalienable rights; men in all countries are entitled to them, not because their ancestors once got together and enumerated them on paper, but because, by repeated negotiations and declarations, all parties are brought to realize them, and of course to believe them to be sacred. Were it necessary, I might show the wisdom of our past conduct, as a people, in not merely comforting ourselves that we were entitled to freedom, but in constantly keeping in view, in addresses, bills of rights, in newspapers, etc. the particular principles on which our freedom must always depend.

It is not merely in this point of view, that I urge the engrafting in the constitution additional declaratory articles. The distinction, in itself just, that all powers not given are reserved, is in effect destroyed by this very constitution, as I shall particularly demonstrate—and even independent of this, the people, by adopting the constitution, give many general undefined powers to congress, in the constitutional exercise of which, the rights in question may be effected. Gentlemen who oppose a federal bill of rights, or further declaratory articles, seem to view the subject in a very narrow imperfect manner. These have for their objects, not only the enumeration of the rights reserved, but principally to explain the general powers delegated in certain material points, and to restrain those who exercise them by fixed known boundaries. Many explanations and restrictions necessary and useful, would be much less so, were the people at large all well and fully acquainted with the principles and affairs of government. There appears to be in the constitution, a studied brevity, and it may also be probable, that several explanatory articles were omitted from a circumstance very common. What we have long and early understood ourselves in the common concerns of the community, we are apt to suppose is understood by others, and need not be expressed; and it is not unnatural or uncommon for the ablest men most frequently to make this mistake. To make declaratory articles unnecessary in an instrument of government, two circumstances must exist; the rights reserved must be indisputably so, and in their nature defined; the powers delegated to the government, must be precisely defined by the words that convey them, and clearly be of such extent and nature as that, by no reasonable construction, they can be made to invade the rights and prerogatives intended to be left in the people.

The first point urged, is, that all power is reserved not expressly given, that particular enumerated powers only are given, that all others are not given, but reserved, and that it is needless to attempt to restrain congress in the exercise of powers they possess not. This reasoning is logical, but of very little importance in the common affairs of men; but the constitution does not appear to respect it even in any view. To prove this, I might cite several clauses in it. I shall only remark on two or three. By art. 1. sect. 9. "No title of nobility shall be granted by congress." Was this clause omitted, what power would congress have to make titles of nobility? in what part of the constitution would they find it? The answer must be, that congress would have no such power—that the people, by adopting the constitution, will not part with it. Why then by a negative clause, restrain congress from doing what it would have no power to do? This clause, then, must have no meaning, or imply, that were it omitted, congress would have the power in question, either upon the principle that some general words in the constitution may be so construed as to give it, or on the principle that congress possesses the powers not expressly reserved. But this clause was in the confederation, and is said to be introduced into the constitution from very great caution. Even a cautionary provision implies a doubt, at least, that it is necessary; and if so in this case, clearly it is also alike necessary in all similar ones. The fact appears to be, that the people in forming the confederation, and the convention, in this instance, acted naturally; they did not leave the point to be settled by general principles and logical inferences; but they settle the point in a few words, and all who read them at once understand them.

The trial by jury in criminal as well as in civil cases, has long been considered as one of our fundamental rights, and has been repeatedly recognized and confirmed by most of the state conventions. But the constitution expressly establishes this trial in criminal, and wholly omits it in civil cases. The jury trial in criminal cases, and the benefit of the writ of habeas corpus, are already as effectually established as any of the fundamental or essential rights of the people in the United States. This being the case, why in adopting a federal constitution do we now establish these, and omit all others, or all others, at least with a few exceptions, such as again agreeing there shall be no *expost facto* laws, no titles of nobility, etc. We must consider this constitution, when adopted, as the supreme act of the people, and in construing it hereafter, we and our posterity must strictly adhere to the letter and spirit of it, and in no instance depart from them: in construing the federal constitution, it will be not only impracticable, but improper to refer to the state constitutions. They are entirely distinct instruments and inferior acts: besides, by the people's now establishing certain fundamental rights, it is strongly implied, that they are of opinion, that they would not otherwise be secured as a part of the federal system, or be regarded in the federal administration as fundamental. Further, these same rights, being established by the state constitutions, and secured to the people, our recognizing them now, implies, that the people thought them insecure by the state establishments, and extinguished or put afloat by the new arrangement of the social system, unless re-established. Further, the people, thus establishing some few rights, and remaining totally silent about others similarly circumstanced, the implication indubitably is, that they mean to relinquish the latter, or at least feel indifferent about them. Rights, therefore, inferred from general principles of reason, being precarious and hardly ascertainable in the common affairs of society, and the people, in forming a federal constitution, explicitly showing they conceive these rights to be thus circumstanced, and accordingly proceeded to enumerate and establish some of them, the conclusion will be, that they have established all which they esteem valuable and sacred. On every principle, then, the people especially having began, ought to go through enumerating, and establish particularly all the rights of individuals, which can by any possibility come in question in making and executing federal laws. I have already observed upon the excellency and importance of the jury trial in civil as well as in criminal cases instead of establishing it in criminal cases only; we ought to establish it generally: instead of the clause of forty or fifty words relative to this subject, why not use the language that has always been used in this country, and say, "the people of the United States shall always be entitled to the trial by jury." This would show the people still hold the right sacred, and enjoin it upon congress substantially to preserve the jury trial in all cases, according to the usage and custom of the country. I have observed before, that it is *the jury trial* we want; the little different appendages and modifications tacked to it in the different states, are no more than a drop in the ocean: the jury trial is a solid uniform feature in a free government; it is the substance we would save, not the little articles of form.

Security against *expost facto* laws, the trial by jury, and the benefits of the writ of habeas corpus, are but a part of those inestimable rights the people of the United States are entitled to, even in judicial proceedings, by the course of the common law. These may be secured in general words, as in New York, the western territory, etc. by declaring the people of the United States shall always be entitled to judicial proceedings according to the course of the common law, as used and established in the said states. Perhaps it would be better to enumerate the particular essential rights the people are entitled to in these proceedings, as has been done in many of the states, and as has been done in England. In this case, the people may proceed to declare, that no man shall be held to answer to any offense, till the same be fully described to him; nor to furnish evidence against himself: that, except in the government of the army and navy, no person shall be tried for any offense, whereby he may incur loss of life, or an infamous punishment, until he be first indicted by a grand jury: that every person shall have a right to produce all proofs that may be favorable to him, and to meet the witnesses against him face to face: that every person shall be entitled to obtain right and justice freely and without delay: that all persons shall have a right to be secure from all unreasonable searches and seizures of their persons, houses, papers, or possessions; and that all warrants shall be deemed contrary to this right, if the foundation of them be not previously supported by oath, and there be not in them a special designation of persons or objects of search, arrest, or seizure: and that no person shall be exiled or molested in his person or effects, otherwise than by the judgment of his peers, or according to the law of the land. A celebrated writer observes upon this last article, that in itself it may be said to comprehend the whole end of political society. These rights are not necessarily reserved, they are established, or enjoyed but in few countries: they are stipulated rights, almost peculiar to British and American laws. In the execution of those laws, individuals, by long custom, by Magna Charta, bills of rights etc., have become entitled to them. A man, at first, by act of parliament, became entitled to the benefits of the writ of habeas corpus—men are entitled to these rights and benefits in the judicial proceedings of our state courts generally: but it will by no means follow, that they will be entitled to them in the federal courts, and have a right to assert them, unless secured and established by the constitution or federal laws. We certainly, in federal processes, might as well claim the benefits of the writ of habeas corpus, as to claim trial by a jury—the right to have council—to have witnesses face to face—to be secure against unreasonable search warrants, etc. was the constitution silent as to the whole of them—but the establishment of the former, will evince that we could not claim them without it; and the omission of the latter, implies they are relinquished, or deemed of no importance. These are rights and benefits individuals acquire by compact; they must claim them under compacts, or immemorial usage—it is doubtful, at least, whether they can be claimed under immemorial usage in this country; and it is, therefore, we generally claim them under compacts, as charters and constitutions.

The people by adopting the federal constitution, give congress general powers to institute a distinct and new judiciary, new courts and to regulate all proceedings in them, under the eight limitations mentioned in a former letter; and the further one, that the benefits of the habeas corpus act shall be enjoyed by individuals. Thus general powers being given to institute courts, and regulate their proceedings, with no provision for securing the rights principally in question, may not congress so exercise those powers, and constitutionally too, as to destroy those rights? Clearly, in my opinion, they are not in any degree secured. But, admitting the case is only doubtful, would it not be prudent and wise to secure them and remove all doubts, since all agree the people ought to enjoy these valuable rights, a very few men excepted, who seem to be rather of opinion that there is little or nothing in them? Were it necessary I might add many observations to show their value and political importance.

The constitution will give congress general powers to raise and support armies. General powers carry with them incidental ones, and the means necessary to the end. In the exercise of these powers, is there any provision in the constitution to prevent the quartering of soldiers on the inhabitants? You will answer, there is not. This may sometimes be deemed a necessary measure in the support of armies; on what principle can the people claim the right to be exempt from this burden? They will urge, perhaps, the practice of the country, and the provisions made in some of the state constitutions—they will be answered, that their claim thus to be exempt is not founded in nature, but only in custom and opinion, or at best, in stipulations in some of the state constitutions, which are local, and inferior in their operation, and can have no control over the general government—that they had adopted a federal constitution—had noticed several rights, but had been totally silent about this exemption—that they had given general powers relative to the subject, which, in their operation, regularly destroyed the claim. Though it is not to be presumed, that we are in any immediate danger from this quarter, yet it is fit and proper to establish, beyond dispute, those rights which are particularly valuable to individuals, and essential to the permanency and duration of free government. An excellent writer observes, that the English, always in possession of their freedom, are frequently unmindful of the value of it: we, at this period, do not seem to be so well off, having, in some instances abused ours; many of us are quite disposed to barter it away for what we call energy, coercion, and some other terms we use as vaguely as that of liberty—There is often as great a rage for change and novelty in politics, as in amusements and fashions.

All parties apparently agree, that the freedom of the press is a fundamental right, and ought not to be restrained by any taxes, duties, or in any manner whatever. Why should not the people, in adopting a federal constitution, declare this, even if there are only doubts about it. But, say the advocates, all powers not given are reserved—true; but the great question is, are not powers given, in the exercise of which this right may be destroyed? The people's or the printer's claim to a free press, is founded on the fundamental laws, that is, compacts, and state constitutions, made by the people. The people, who can annihilate or alter those constitutions, can annihilate or limit this right. This may be done by giving general powers, as well as by using particular words. No right claimed under a state constitution, will avail against a law of the union, made in pursuance of the federal constitution: therefore the question is, what laws will congress have a right to make by the constitution of the union, and particularly touching the press? By art. 1. sect. 8. congress will have power to lay and collect taxes, duties, imposts and excise. By this congress will clearly have power to lay and collect all kind of taxes whatever—taxes on houses, lands, polls, industry, merchandise, etc.—taxes on deeds, bonds, and all written instruments—on writs, pleas, and all judicial proceedings, on licences, naval officers' papers, etc. on newspapers, advertisements, etc. and to require bonds of the naval officers, clerks, printers, etc. to account for the taxes that may become due on papers that go through their hands. Printing, like all other business, must cease when taxed beyond its profits; and it appears to me, that a power to tax the press at discretion, is a power to destroy or restrain the freedom of it. There may be other powers given, in the exercise of which this freedom may be affected; and certainly it is of too much importance to be left thus liable to be taxed, and constantly to constructions and inferences. A free press is the channel of communication as to mercantile and public affairs; by means of it the people in large countries ascertain each others' sentiments; are enabled to unite, and become formidable to those rulers who adopt improper measures. Newspapers may sometimes be the vehicles of abuse, and of many things not true; but these are but small inconveniences, in my mind, among many advantages. A celebrated writer I have several times quoted, speaking in high terms of the English liberties, says, "lastly the key stone was put to the arch, by the final establishment of the freedom of the press." I shall not dwell longer upon the fundamental rights, to some of which I have attended in this letter, for the same reasons that these I have mentioned, ought to be expressly secured, lest in the exercise of general powers given they may be invaded: it is pretty clear, that some other of less importance, or less in danger, might with propriety also be secured.

I shall now proceed to examine briefly the powers proposed to be vested in the several branches of the government, and especially the mode of levying and collecting internal taxes.

The Federal Farmer

LETTER XVII

January 23, 1788.

Dear Sir,

I believe the people of the United States are full in the opinion, that a free and mild government can be preserved in their extensive territories, only under the substantial forms of a federal republic. As several of the ablest advocates for the system proposed, have acknowledged this (and I hope the confessions they have published will be preserved and remembered) I shall not take up time to establish this point. A question then arises, how far that system partakes of a federal republic. I observed in a former letter, that it appears to be the first important step to a consolidation of the states; that its strong tendency is to that point.

But what do we mean by a federal republic and what by a consolidated government? To erect a federal republic, we must first make a number of states on republican principles; each state with a government organized for the internal management of its affairs: The states, as such, must unite under a federal head, and delegate to it powers to make and execute laws in certain enumerated cases, under certain restrictions; this head may be a single assembly, like the present congress, or the Amphictionic council; or it may consist of a legislature, with one or more branches; of an executive, and of a judiciary. To form a consolidated, or one entire government, there must be no state, or local governments, but all things, persons and property, must be subject to the laws of one legislature alone; to one executive, and one judiciary. Each state government, as the government of New Jersey etc., is a consolidated, or one entire government, as it respects the counties, towns, citizens, and property within the limits of the state. The state governments are the basis, the pillar on which the federal head is placed, and the whole together, when formed on elective principles, constitutes a federal republic. A federal republic in itself supposes state or local governments to exist, as the body or props, on which the federal head rests, and that it cannot remain a moment after they cease. In erecting the federal government, and always in its councils, each state must be known as a sovereign body; but in erecting this government, I conceive, the legislature of the state, by the expressed or implied assent of the people, or the people of the state, under the direction of the government of it, may accede to the federal compact: Nor do I conceive it to be necessarily a part of a confederacy of states, that each have an equal voice in the general councils. A confederated republic being organized, each state must retain powers for managing its internal police, and all delegate to the union power to mange general concerns: The quantity of power the union must possess is one thing, the mode of exercising the powers given, is quite a different consideration; and it is the mode of exercising them, that makes one of the essential distinctions between one entire or consolidated government, and a federal republic; that is, however the government may be organized, if the laws of the union, in most important concerns, as in levying and collecting taxes, raising troops, etc. operate immediately upon the persons and property of individuals, and not on states, extend to organizing the militia, etc. the government, as to its administration, as to making and executing laws, is not federal, but consolidated. To illustrate my idea—the union makes a requisition, and assigns to each state its quota of men or monies wanted; each state, by its own laws and officers, in its own way, furnishes its quota: here the state governments stand between the union and individuals; the laws of the union operate only on states, as such, and federally: Here nothing can be done without the meetings of the state legislatures—but in the other case the union, though the state legislatures should not meet for years together, proceeds immediately, by its own laws and officers, to levy and collect monies of individuals, to enlist men, form armies, etc. Here the laws of the union operate immediately on the body of the people, on persons and property; in the same manner the laws of one entire consolidated government operate—These two modes are very distinct, and in their operation and consequences have directly opposite tendencies: The first makes the existence of the state governments indispensable, and throws all the detail business of levying and collecting the taxes, etc. into the hands of those governments, and into the hands, of course, of many thousand officers solely created by and dependent on the state. The last entirely excludes the agency of the respective states, and throws the whole business of levying and collecting taxes, etc. into the hands of many thousand officers solely created by, and dependent upon the union, and makes the existence of the state government of no consequence in the case. It is true, congress in raising any given sum in direct taxes, must by the constitution, raise so much of it in one state, and so much in another, by a fixed rule, which most of the states some time since agreed to: But this does not affect the principle in question, it only secures each state against any arbitrary proportions. The federal mode is perfectly safe and eligible, founded in the true spirit of a confederated republic; there could be no possible exception to it, did we not find by experience, that the states will sometimes neglect to comply with the reasonable requisitions of the union. It being according to the fundamental principles of federal republics, to raise men and monies by requisitions, and for the states individually to organize and train the militia, I conceive, there can be no reason whatever for departing from them, except this, that the states sometimes neglect to comply with reasonable requisitions, and that it is dangerous to attempt to compel a delinquent state by force, as it may often produce a war. We ought, therefore, to inquire attentively, how extensive the evils to be guarded against are, and cautiously limit the remedies to the extent of the evils. I am not about to defend the confederation, or to charge the proposed constitution with imperfections not in it; but we ought to examine facts, and strip them of the false colorings often given them by incautious observations, by unthinking or designing men. We ought to premise, that laws for raising men and monies, even in consolidated governments, are not often punctually complied with. Historians, except in extraordinary cases, very seldom take notice of the detail collection of taxes; but these facts we have fully proved, and well attested; that the most energetic governments have relinquished taxes frequently, which were of many years standing. These facts amply prove, that taxes assessed, have remained many years uncollected. I agree there have been instances in the republics of Greece, Holland, etc. in the course of several centuries, of states neglecting to pay their quotas of requisitions; but it is a circumstance certainly deserving of attention, whether these nations which have depended on requisitions principally for their defense, have not raised men and monies nearly as punctually as entire governments, which have taxed directly; whether we have not found the latter as often distressed for the want of troops and monies, as the former. It has been said that the Amphictionic council, and the Germanic head, have not possessed sufficient powers to control the members of the republic in a proper manner. Is this, if true, to be imputed to requisitions? Is it not principally to be imputed to the unequal powers of those members, connected with this important circumstance, that each member possessed power to league itself with foreign powers, and powerful neighbors, without the consent of the head? After all, has not the Germanic body a government as good as its neighbors in general? And did not the Grecian republic remain united several centuries, and form the theater of human greatness? No government in Europe has commanded monies more plentifully than the government of Holland. As to the United States, the separate states lay taxes directly, and the union calls for taxes by way of requisitions; and is it a fact, that more monies are due in proportion on requisitions in the United States, than on the state taxes directly laid? It is only about ten years since congress began to make requisitions, and in that time, the monies, etc. required, and the bounties given for men required of the states, have amounted, specie value, to about 36 million dollars, about 24 millions of dollars of which have been actually paid; and a very considerable part of the 12 millions not paid, remains so not so much from the neglect of the states, as from the sudden changes in paper money, etc. which in a great measure rendered payments of no service, and which often induced the union indirectly to relinquish one demand, by making another in a different form. Before we totally condemn requisitions, we ought to consider what immense bounties the states gave, and what prodigious exertions they made in the war, in order to comply with the requisitions of congress; and if since the peace they have been delinquent, ought we not carefully to inquire, whether that delinquency is to be imputed solely to the nature of requisitions? Ought it not in part to be imputed to two other causes? I mean first, an opinion, that has extensively prevailed, that the requisitions for domestic interest have not been founded on just principles; and secondly, the circumstance, that the government itself, by proposing imposts, etc. has departed virtually from the constitutional system; which proposed changes, like all changes proposed in government, produce an inattention and negligence in the execution of the government in being.

I am not for depending wholly on requisitions; but I mention these few facts to show they are not so totally futile as many pretend. For the truth of many of these facts I appeal to the public records; and for the truth of the others, I appeal to many republic characters, who are best informed in the affairs of the United States. Since the peace, and till the convention reported, the wisest men in the United States generally supposed, that certain limited funds would answer the purposes of the union: and though the states are by no means in so good a condition as I wish they were, yet, I think, I may very safely affirm, they are in a better condition than they would be had congress always possessed the powers of taxation now contended for. The fact is admitted, that our federal government does not possess sufficient powers to give life and vigor to the political system; and that we experience disappointments, and several inconveniences; but we ought carefully to distinguish those which are merely the consequences of a severe and tedious war, from those which arise from defects in the federal system. There has been an entire revolution in the United States within thirteen years, and the least we can compute the waste of labor and property at, during that period, by the war, is three hundred million of dollars. Our people are like a man just recovering from a severe fit of sickness. It was the war that disturbed the course of commerce, introduced floods of paper money, the stagnation of credit, and threw may valuable men out of steady business. From these sources our greatest evils arise; men of knowledge and reflection must perceive it; but then, have we not done more in three or four years past, in repairing the injuries of the war, by repairing houses and estates, restoring industry, frugality, the fisheries, manufactures, etc. and thereby laying the foundation of good government, and of individual and political happiness, than any people ever did in a like time; we must judge from a view of the country and facts, and not from foreign newspapers, or our own, which are printed chiefly in the commercial towns, where imprudent living, imprudent importations, and many unexpected disappointments have produced a despondency and a disposition to view every thing on the dark side. Some of the evils we feel, all will agree, ought to be imputed to the defective administration of the governments. From these and various considerations, I am very clearly of opinion, that the evils we sustain, merely on account of the defects of the confederation, are but as a feather in the balance against a mountain, compared with those which would, infallibly, be the result of the loss of general liberty, and that happiness men enjoy under a frugal, free and mild government.

Heretofore we do not seem to have seen danger anywhere, but in giving power to congress, and now nowhere but in congress wanting powers; and, without examining the extent of the evils to be remedied, by one step, we are for giving up to congress almost all powers of any importance without limitation. The defects of the confederation are extravagantly magnified, and every species of pain we feel imputed to them: and hence it is inferred, there must be a total change of the principles, as well as forms of government: and in the main point, touching the federal powers, we rest all on a logical inference, totally inconsistent with experience and sound political reasoning.

It is said, that as the federal head must make peace and war, and provide for the common defense, it ought to possess all powers necessary to that end: that powers unlimited, as to the purse and sword, to raise men and monies, and form the militia, are necessary to that end; and, therefore, the federal head ought to possess them. This reasoning is far more specious than solid: it is necessary that these powers so exist in the body politic, as to be called into exercise whenever necessary for the public safety; but it is by no means true, that the man, or congress of men, whose duty it more immediately is to provide for the common defense, ought to possess them without limitation. But clear it is, that if such men, or congress, be not in a situation to hold them without danger to liberty, he or they ought not to possess them. It has long been thought to be a well-founded position, that the purse and sword ought not to be placed in the same hands in a free government. Our wise ancestors have carefully separated them—placed the sword in the hands of their king, even under considerable limitations, and the purse in the hands of the commons alone: yet the king makes peace and war, and it is his duty to provide for the common defense of the nation. This authority at least goes thus far—that a nation, well versed in the science of government, does not conceive it to be necessary or expedient for the man entrusted with the common defense and general tranquility, to possess unlimitedly the powers in question, or even in any considerable degree. Could he, whose duty it is to defend the public, possess in himself independently, all the means of doing it consistent with the public good, it might be convenient: but the people of England know that their liberties and happiness would be in infinitely greater danger from the king's unlimited possession of these powers, than from all external enemies and internal commotions to which they might be exposed: therefore, though they have made it his duty to guard the empire, yet they have wisely placed in other hands, the hands of their representatives, the power to deal out and control the means. In Holland their high mightinesses must provide for the common defense, but for the means they depend, in a considerable degree, upon requisitions made on the state or local assemblies. Reason and facts evince that however convenient it might be for an executive magistrate, or federal head, more immediately charged with the national defense and safety, solely, directly, and independently to possess all the means; yet such magistrate, or head, never ought to possess them, if thereby the public liberties shall be endangered. The powers in question never have been, by nations wise and free, deposited, nor can they ever be, with safety, anywhere, but in the principal members of the national system; where these form one entire government, as in Great Britain, they are separated and lodged in the principal members of it. But in a federal republic, there is quite a different organization; the people form this kind of government, generally, because their territories are too extensive to admit of their assembling in one legislature, or of executing the laws on free principles under one entire government. They convene in their local assemblies, for local purposes, and for managing their internal concerns, and unite their states under a federal head for general purposes. It is the essential characteristic of a confederated republic, that this head be dependent on, and kept within limited bounds by, the local governments; and it is because, in these alone, in fact, the people can be substantially assembled or represented. It is, therefore, we very universally see, in this kind of government, the congressional powers placed in a few hands, and accordingly limited, and specifically enumerated: and the local assemblies strong and well-guarded, and composed of numerous members. Wise men will always place the controlling power where the people are substantially collected by their representatives. By the proposed system, the federal head will possess, without limitation, almost every species of power that can, in its exercise, tend to change the government, or to endanger liberty; while in it, I think it has been fully shown, the people will have but the shadow of representation, and but the shadow of security for their rights and liberties. In a confederated republic, the division of representation, etc. in its nature, requires a correspondent division and deposit of powers relative to taxes and military concerns: and I think the plan offered stands quite alone, in confounding the principles of governments in themselves totally distinct. I wish not to exculpate the states for their improper neglect in not paying their quotas of requisitions; but, in applying the remedy, we must be governed by reason and facts. It will not be denied, that the people have a right to change the government when the majority choose it, if not restrained by some existing compact—that they have a right to displace their rulers, and consequently to determine when their measures are reasonable or not—and that they have a right, at any time, to put a stop to those measures they may deem prejudicial to them, by such forms and negatives as they may see fit to provide. From all these, and many other well-founded considerations, I need not mention, a question arises, what powers shall there be delegated to the federal head, to insure safety, as well as energy, in the government? I think there is a safe and proper medium pointed out by experience, by reason, and facts. When we have organized the government, we ought to give power to the union, so far only as experience and present circumstances shall direct, with a reasonable regard to time to come. Should future circumstances, contrary to our expectations, require that further powers be transferred to the union, we can do it far more easily, than get back those we may now imprudently give. The system proposed is untried: candid advocates and opposers admit, that it is, in a degree, a mere experiment, and that its organization is weak and imperfect; surely then, the safe ground is cautiously to vest power in it, and when we are sure we have given enough for ordinary exigencies, to be extremely careful how we delegate powers, which, in common cases, must necessarily be useless or abused, and of very uncertain effect in uncommon ones.

By giving the union power to regulate commerce, and to levy and collect taxes by imposts, we give it an extensive authority, and permanent productive funds, I believe quite as adequate to the present demands of the union, as excises and direct taxes can be made to the present demands of the separate states. The state governments are now about four times as expensive as that of the union; and their several state debts added together, are nearly as large as that of the union—Our impost duties since the peace have been almost as productive as the other sources of taxation, and when under one general system of regulations, the probability is, that those duties will be very considerably increased. Indeed the representation proposed will hardly justify giving to congress unlimited powers to raise taxes by imposts, in addition to the other powers the union must necessarily have. It is said, that if congress possess only authority to raise taxes by imposts, trade probably will be overburdened with taxes, and the taxes of the union be found inadequate to any uncommon exigencies: To this we may observe, that trade generally finds its own level, and will naturally and necessarily leave off any undue burdens laid upon it: further, if congress alone possess the impost, and also unlimited power to raise monies by excises and direct taxes, there must be much more danger that two taxing powers, the union and states, will carry excises and direct taxes to an unreasonable extent, especially as these have not the natural boundaries taxes on trade have. However, it is not my object to propose to exclude congress from raising monies by internal taxes, as by duties, excises, and direct taxes; but my opinion is, that congress, especially in its proposed organization, ought not to raise monies by internal taxes, except in strict conformity to the federal plan; that is, by the agency of the state governments in all cases, except where a state shall neglect, for an unreasonable time, to pay its quota of a requisition; and never where so many of the state legislatures as represent a majority of the people, shall formally determine an excise law or requisition is improper, in their next session after the same be laid before them. We ought always to recollect that the evil to be guarded against is found by our own experience, and the experience of others, to be mere neglect in the states to pay their quotas; and power in the union to levy and collect the neglecting states' quota, with interest, is fully adequate to the evil. By this federal plan, with this exception mentioned, we secure the means of collecting the taxes by the usual process of law, and avoid the evil of attempting to compel or coerce a state; and we avoid also a circumstance, which never yet could be, and I am fully confident never can be, admitted in a free federal republic; I mean a permanent and continued system of tax laws of the union, executed in the bowels of the states by many thousand officers, dependent as to the assessing and collecting federal taxes, solely upon the union. On every principle, then, we ought to provide, that the union render an exact account of all monies raised by imposts and other taxes; and that whenever monies shall be wanted for the purposes of the union, beyond the proceeds of the impost duties, requisitions shall be made on the states for the monies so wanted; and that the power of laying and collecting shall never be exercised, except in cases where a state shall neglect, a given time, to pay its quota. This mode seems to be strongly pointed out by the reason of the case, and spirit of the government; and I believe, there is no instance to be found in a federal republic, where the congressional powers ever extended generally to collecting monies by direct taxes or excises. Creating all these restrictions, still the powers of the union in matters of taxation, will be too unlimited; further checks, in my mind, are indispensably necessary. Nor do I conceive, that as full a representation as is practicable in the federal government, will afford sufficient security: the strength of the government, and the confidence of the people, must be collected principally in the local assemblies; every part or branch of the federal head must be feeble, and unsafely trusted with large powers. A government possessed of more power than its constituent parts will justify, will not only probably abuse it, but be unequal to bear its own burden; it may as soon be destroyed by the pressure of power, as languish and perish for want of it.

There are two ways further of raising checks, and guarding against undue combinations and influence in a federal system. The first is, in levying taxes, raising and keeping up armies, in building navies, in forming plans for the militia, and in appropriating monies for the support of the military, to require the attendance of a large proportion of the federal representatives, as two-thirds or three-fourths of them; and in passing laws, in these important cases, to require the consent of two-thirds or three-fourths of the members present. The second is, by requiring that certain important laws of the federal head, as a requisition or a law of raising monies by excise, shall be laid before the state legislatures, and if disapproved of by a given number of them, say by as many of them as represent a majority of the people, the law shall have no effect. Whether it would be advisable to adopt both, or either of these checks, I will not undertake to determine. We have seen them both exist in confederated republics. The first exists substantially in the confederation, and will exist in some measure in the plan proposed, as in choosing a president by the house, in expelling members; in the senate, in making treaties, and in deciding on impeachments, and in the whole in altering the constitution. The last exists in the United Netherlands, but in a much greater extent. The first is founded on this principle, that these important measures may, sometimes, be adopted by a bare quorum of members, perhaps, from a few states, and that a bare majority of the federal representatives may frequently be of the aristocracy, or some particular interests, connections, or parties in the community, and governed by motives, views, and inclinations not compatible with the general interest. The last is founded on this principle, that the people will be substantially represented, only in their state or local assemblies; that their principal security must be found in them; and that, therefore, they ought to have ultimately a constitutional control over such interesting measures.

I have often heard it observed, that our people are well-informed, and will not submit to oppressive governments; that the state governments will be their ready advocates, and possess their confidence, mix with them, and enter into all their wants and feelings. This is all true; but of what avail will these circumstances be, if the state governments, thus allowed to be the guardians of the people, possess no kind of power by the forms of the social compact, to stop in their passage, the laws of congress injurious to the people. State governments must stand and see the law take place; they may complain and petition—so may individuals; the members of them, in extreme cases, may resist, on the principles of self-defense—so may the people and individuals.

It has been observed, that the people, in extensive territories, have more power, compared with that of their rulers, than in small states. Is not directly the opposite true? The people in a small state can unite and act in concert, and with vigour; but in large territories, the men who govern find it more easy to unite, while people cannot; while they cannot collect the opinions of each part, while they move to different points, and one part is often played off against the other.

It has been asserted, that the confederate head of a republic at best, is in general weak and dependent—that the people will attach themselves to, and support their local governments, in all disputes with the union. Admit the fact: is it any way to remove the inconvenience by accumulating powers upon a weak organization? The fact is, that the detail administration of affairs, in this mixed republic, depends principally on the local governments; and the people would be wretched without them: and a great proportion of social happiness depends on the internal administration of justice, and on internal police. The splendor of the monarch, and the power of the government are one thing. The happiness of the subject depends on very different causes: but it is to the latter, that the best men, the greatest ornaments of human nature, have most carefully attended: it is to the former tyrants and oppressors have always aimed.

The Federal Farmer

A Note on the Type

The typeface used in this book is Adobe Caslon, a modern interpretation of the classic faces cut in the 1720s by the English typographer William Caslon (1692–1766). Caslon was trained as an engraver but turned increasingly to type design and cutting, setting up his own type foundry in 1720. Caslon's design became the first major native English typeface to achieve wide popularity. It displays the small lowercase height and the relatively restrained contrast typical of what are now called "old style" fonts. Modern taste and technology have smoothed out many of the idiosyncrasies of William Caslon's original cutting, but the modern version retains some of the warmth and much of the straightforward honesty that have made Caslon a good and dependable friend of the typographer for more than 250 years.

This book is printed on paper that is acid-free and meets the requirements of the American National Standard for Permanence of Paper for Printed Library Materials, Z39.48-1992. ♾

Book design by Martin Lubin Graphic Design, New York, New York

Typography by WorldComp, Sterling, Virginia

Printed and bound by Worzalla Publishing Company, Stevens Point, Wisconsin